No. 5 -

Frederic B. Ripley

NEW ILLUSTRATED JUVENILES.

AUNT FANNY'S STORY BOOK. Illustrated. 16mo. - $0 50
THE CHILD'S PRESENT. Illustrated. 16mo.
HOWITT'S PICTURE AND VERSE BOOK. Illustrated with 100 plates. 75 cts.; gilt - 1 00
HOME FOR THE HOLIDAYS. Illustrated. 4to., 25 cts.; cloth 50
STORY OF JOAN OF ARC. By R. M. Evans. With 23 illustrations. 16mo. - 75
ROBINSON CRUSOE. Pictorial Edition. 300 plates. 8vo. - 1 50
THE CARAVAN; A COLLECTION OF TALES AND STORIES FROM THE GERMAN. Translated by G. P. Quackenboss. Illustrated by Orr. 16mo.
INNOCENCE OF CHILDHOOD. By Mrs. Colman. Illustrated 50
HOME RECREATIONS, comprising Travels and Adventures, &c. Colored Illustrations. 16mo. 87
FIRESIDE FAIRIES. A New Story Book. My Miss Susan Pindar. Finely Illustrated. 16mo.
STORY OF LITTLE JOHN. Trans. from the French. Illus. 62
LIVES AND ANECDOTES OF ILLUSTRIOUS MEN. 16mo. 75
UNCLE JOHN'S PANORAMIC PICTURE BOOKS. Six kinds, 25 cts. each; half-cloth - 50
HOLIDAY HOUSE. Tales, by Catherine Sinclair. Illustrated 75
PUSS IN BOOTS. Finely illus. by O. Speckter. 50c.; ex. glt. - 75
TALES AND STORIES for Boys and Girls. By Mary Howitt 75
AMERICAN HISTORICAL TALES for Youth. 16mo. - 75

LIBRARY FOR MY YOUNG COUNTRYMEN.

ADVENTURES of Captain John Smith. By the Author of Uncle Philip - 38
ADVENTURES of Daniel Boon. By do. - 38
DAWNINGS of Genius. By Anne Pratt - 38
LIFE and Adventures of Henry Hudson. By the Author of Uncle Philip - 38
LIFE and Adventures of Hernan Cortez. By do. - 38
PHILIP RANDOLPH. A Tale of Virginia. By Mary Gertrude. 38
ROWAN'S History of the French Revolution. 2 vols. - 75
SOUTHEY'S Life of Cromwell - 38

TALES FOR THE PEOPLE AND THEIR CHILDREN.

ALICE FRANKLIN. By Mary Howitt - $0 38
LOVE AND MONEY. By do. - 38
HOPE ON, HOPE EVER! Do. 38
LITTLE COIN, MUCH CARE. By do. - 38
MY OWN STORY. By do. - 38
MY UNCLE, THE CLOCKMAKER. By do. - 38
NO SENSE LIKE COMMON SENSE. By do. - 38
SOWING AND REAPING. Do. 38
STRIVE AND THRIVE. By do. 38
THE TWO APPRENTICES. By do. - 38
WHICH IS THE WISER? Do. 38
WHO SHALL BE GREATEST? By do. - 38
WORK AND WAGES. By do. 38
CROFTON BOYS, The. By Harriet Martineau - 38
DANGERS OF DINING OUT. By Mrs. Ellis - 38
FIRST IMPRESSIONS. By do. 38
MINISTER'S FAMILY. By do. 38
SOMMERVILLE HALL. By do. 38
DOMESTIC TALES. By Hannah More. 2 vols. - 75
EARLY FRIENDSHIP. By Mrs. Copley - 38
FARMER'S DAUGHTER, The. By Mrs. Cameron - 38
LOOKING-GLASS FOR THE MIND. Many plates - 45
MASTERMAN READY. By Capt. Marryat. 3 vols. - 1 2
PEASANT AND THE PRINCE. By H. Martineau - 38
POPLAR GROVE. By Mrs. Copley - 38
SETTLERS IN CANADA. By Capt. Marryatt. 2 vols. - 75
TIRED OF HOUSEKEEPING. By T. S. Arthur - 38
TWIN SISTERS, The. By Mrs. Sandham - 38
YOUNG STUDENT. By Madame Guizot. 3 vols. - 1 1

SECOND SERIES.

CHANCES AND CHANGES. By Charles Burdett - 38
NEVER TOO LATE. By do. - 38
GOLDMAKER'S VILLAGE. By H. Zschokke - 38
OCEAN WORK, ANCIENT AND MODERN. By J. H. Wright - 38
THE MISSION; or, Scenes in Africa. By Capt. Marryatt. 2 vols. 75
STORY OF A GENIUS - 38

D. Appleton & Co.'s Publications.

HISTORICAL AND BIOGRAPHICAL WORKS.

ARNOLD, (Dr.) Early History of Rome. 2 vols. 8vo. - - $5 00
ARNOLD, (Dr.) History of the Later Roman Commonwealth. 8vo. - - - - - - 2 50
ARNOLD, (Dr.) Lectures on Modern History, edited by Professor Reed. 12mo. - - - 1 25
ARNOLD, (Dr.) Life and Correspondence, by the Rev. A. P. Stanley. 2d ed. 8vo. - - 2 00
BURNETT'S History of the Northwestern Territory. 8vo. - - 2 50
CARLYLE'S Life of Schiller. A new edition. 12mo. - - - 75
COIT'S History of Puritanism. 12mo. - - - - - - 1 00
EVELYN'S Life of Mrs. Godolphin, edited by Bishop of Oxford. 12mo - - - - - 50
FROST (Professor) History of the United States Navy. Plates. 12mo. 1 00
FROST, (Professor) History of the United States Army. Plates. 12mo. - - - - - - 1 00
FROST, (Professor) History of the Indians of North America. Plates. 12mo. - - - - - - 1 00
FROST, (Professor) History of the Colonies of America. 12mo. Illustrated - - - - - 1 00
FROST, (Professor) Life of Gen. Zachary Taylor. 12mo. Illustrated. - - - - - - 1 25
GUIZOT'S History of Civilization in Europe, edited by Professor Henry. 12mo - - - 1 00
GUIZOT'S Complete History of Civilization, translated by Hazlett. 4 vols. - - - - 3 50
GUIZOT'S History of the English Revolution, 1640. 12mo. - - 1 25
GAYARRE'S Romance of the History of Louisiana. 12mo. - - 1 00
HULL, (General) Military and Civil Life. 8vo - - - - 2 00
KING, (Colonel) History of the Argentine Republic. 12mo. - 75
KOHLRAUSCH'S Complete History of Germany. 8vo. - - 1 50
MAHON'S (Lord) History of England, edited by Professor Reed. 2 vols. 8vo - - - - - 5 00
MICHELET'S History of France from the Earliest Period. 2 vols. 5 50
MICHELET'S History of the Roman Republic. 12mo. - - 90
MICHELET'S History of the People. 12mo. - - - - 63

MICHELET'S Life of Martin Luther. 12mo. - - - - 90
NAPOLEON, Life of, from the French of Laurent De L'Ardeche. 2 vols. 8vo. 500 cuts - 4 00
O'CALLAGHAN'S Early History of New York. 2 vols. 8vo. - 5 00
ROWAN'S History of the French Revolution. 18mo. 2 vols. in 1 63
SEWELL'S Child's History of Rome. 8mo. - - - - 50
SOUTHEY'S Life of Oliver Cromwell. 18mo. - - - - 38
SPRAGUE'S History of the Florida War. Map and Plates. 8vo. 2 50
STEVEN'S History of Georgia. vol. 1 - - - - - 2 50
TAYLOR'S Natural History of Society in the Barbarous and Civilized State. 2 vols. 12mo. - 2 25
TAYLOR'S Manual of Ancient and Modern History. Edited by Professor Henry. 8vo. - - 2 50
TAYLOR'S Ancient History—Separate - - - - - 1 25
TAYLOR'S Modern History—Separate - - - - - 1 50
Used as a Text-book in several Colleges.
TWISS. History of the Oregon Territory. 12mo. - - - 75

LAW BOOKS.

ANTHON'S Law Student; or, Guides to the Study of the Law in its Principles.
HOLCOMBE'S Digest of the Decisions of the Supreme Court of the U. S., from its Commencement to the present time. Large 8vo., law sheep - - - 6 00
HOLCOMBE'S Supreme Court Leading Cases on Commercial Law. 8vo. law sheep - 4 00
HOLCOMBE'S Law of Debtor and Creditor in the United States and Canada. 8vo. - - - 3 50
SMITH'S Compendium of Mercantile Law. With Large American Additions, by Holcombe and Gholson. 8vo., law sheep - 4 00
These volumes are highly commended by Justices Taney and Woodbury, Daniel Webster, Rufus Choate, and Chancellor Kent, &c.
WARREN'S Popular and Practical Introduction to Law Studies. With American additions, by Thomas W. Clerke. 8vo., law sheep - - - - - 3 50

THE
ADVENTURES
OF THE
CONQUEROR OF MEXICO

By the Author of
"Uncle Philip's Conversations"

NEW YORK
D. Appleton & Company, 200 Broadway

THE ADVENTURES OF HERNAN CORTES,

THE CONQUEROR OF MEXICO.

BY THE AUTHOR OF "UNCLE PHILIP'S CONVERSATIONS."

NEW YORK:
D. APPLETON & CO., 200 BROADWAY.
PHILADELPHIA:
GEORGE S. APPLETON, 164 CHESTNUT ST.

M DCCC LI.

Entered, according to Act of Congress, in the year 1843,
By D. APPLETON & CO.,
in the Clerk's Office of the District Court of the United States, for the Southern District of New York.

TO

THOSE OF MY YOUNG COUNTRYMEN,

WHO ARE DISPOSED TO GATHER FROM THE PAGES OF
HISTORY, A STORY OF REAL LIFE, STRANGER
THAN ANY TALE OF ROMANCE,

This Volume

IS AFFECTIONATELY DEDICATED,

BY THE AUTHOR.

NOTE.

The writer of this volume has thought it best not to encumber a book written for the young, with references to authorities. He owes it to himself, however, to say, that he believes he has made no statement for which authority may not readily be produced.

To any older readers, who may possibly glance at the volume, he would remark, that he is indebted for his materials principally to Antonio de Herrera, Bernal Diaz, Antonio de Solis, Torquemada, Clavigero, Don Telesforo de Trueba y Cosio, Venegas, the letters of Hernan Cortes, the English historian Robertson, and our own lamented countryman, R. C. Sands, Esq.

CONTENTS.

CHAPTER I.

Birth and parentage of Hernan Cortes—His early boyhood—At the age of fourteen he is sent to the University of Salamanca—Proves lazy, and returns home—Leaves his books, and takes to field-sports—Disappointment of his father—Passion of young Cortes for military life—Determines to join the great captain Gonzalo in the wars of Italy, but is disappointed—Resolves to accompany his kinsman Ovando to Hispaniola, but is prevented by an accident—At length reaches Hispaniola in 1504—Kindness of Ovando—Restlessness of Cortes—His third disappointment—Accompanies Diego Velasquez in his conquest of Cuba—Imprudence of Cortes—Expedition of Hernandez de Cordova and Juan de Grijalva—Discoveries of Grijalva—Excitement among the Spaniards—Cortes manages to get command of an expedition for the continent—Jealousy of Velasquez—Attempts to stop him at Trinidad and Havana—Enthusiasm among the followers of Cortes . . . . . . Page 13

CHAPTER II.

Cortes arrives at Cozumel—Imprudence of Alvarado—Discovery of Geronimo de Aguilar—his wretched condition—The fleet reaches Tabasco—Hostility of the natives—Cortes offers to treat with them; they refuse—Notwithstanding their opposition, he makes his landing—Defeats them on the great plain of Ceutla—Receives Dona Marina as a present—He erects a cross upon the plain—The fleet sails for St. Juan de Ulua—Reaches that harbor—Kindness of the natives—Interview with Teutchlile, their chief—Demands that he may see the Emperor Montezuma, and sends presents to him—Alarm of Montezuma—He refuses to see the strangers, but sends presents to them—Cortes again demands to see him—Anger and fear of the Emperor—Commands Cortes to leave his empire, yet sends him further presents . . 31

CHAPTER III.

Teutchlile arrives at the Spanish camp with the commands of Montezuma—Finds Cortes in the midst of difficulties with his men—Leaves the camp angry—Murmurs of the men—Management of Cortes—Commences the settlement of Villa Rica de la Vera Cruz—Quiets the complaints of the discontented—The Cacique of Chempoalla invites him to visit him—Cortes accepts the invitation—Interview between them—The settlement is removed to Quiabislan—Friendship of the Caciques of Chempoalla and Quiabislan—The tax-gatherers of Montezuma arrive—Cortes arrests them—The Totonacas become his friends—Visits the Cincapacingas—Makes friends of them—Imprudence of Cortes in the temple of Chempoalla—Sends messengers with presents to the King of Spain—Plot of Escudero and Centeno to stop them—They are put to death—Cortes destroys his fleet, and prepares to march toward Mexico—Arrival of Alonzo de Pineda upon the coast—Stratagem of Cortes—Sets out on his march—Passes Xalapan, Socachema, and Texotla, and arrives at Xocotlan—Interview with the Cacique—Determines to pursue his journey through the province of Tlascala . . . 46

CHAPTER IV.

Cortes enters the Tlascalan territory—Character of the people—Wars with the Tlascalans—Cortes subdues them—They become his allies—Marches to Cholula—Conspiracy and awful massacre of the Cholulans 64

CHAPTER V.

Cortes sends messengers to Montezuma, and leaves Cholula—Alarm of Montezuma—The Spaniards reach the summit of Ithualco, and see the valley of Mexico—Montezuma retires to the palace of Tlillancalmecatl to mourn and pray—Sends his nephew Cacamatzin to dissuade Cortes from entering his city—Cortes crosses the causeway of Iztapalapan—Meets Montezuma—His splendid appearance—Enters Mexico, and makes his quarters at the palace of Axajacatl—Montezuma visits him—Cortes returns the visit—By his permission, visits the great market-place, the temple, &c.—Is disgusted in the temple—Anger of Montezuma—Suspicions of the Tlascalans—Death of Escalante—Treachery of the nobles—Cortes resolves to seize Montezuma—Enters his palace, and carries him away to the Spanish quarters 83

CHAPTER VI.

Montezuma becomes satisfied at the Spanish quarters—Arrival of Quauhpopoca—He is delivered to Cortes—His confession—Is tried, and condemned to die—Montezuma is fettered, and Quauhpopoca burnt—Revolt of Cacamatzin, the lord of Tezcuco—He is made a prisoner—Cortes persuades Montezuma to swear allegiance to the King of Spain—and to send him a present of gold and silver—The nobles are roused—Montezuma orders Cortes to leave the country—allows him time to build ships for his departure—Arrival of Pamphilo de Narvaez with eighteen ships—Cortes is ordered again to leave—His joy and disappointment—Treachery of Montejo—Anger of Velasquez—Endeavors to make a friend of Narvaez—Sends him messages and presents—Narvaez proves stubborn—Cortes leaves one hundred and fifty men with Alvarado at Mexico, and marches to Chempoalla—Attacks him at midnight and makes him a prisoner—The soldiers of Narvaez gladly enlist under him . . 102

CHAPTER VII.

Insurrection of the Mexicans in the capital—Struggles of Cortes—Death of Montezuma—Awful conflict in the temple—The Spaniards retreat from Mexico—Dreadful massacre on the causeway of Tacuba—Cortes escapes with the remnant of his army to the temple of Otoncalpolco—Determines to go to Tlascala 120

CHAPTER VIII.

Battle of Otompan—Victory of the Spaniards—Cortes reaches Tlascala—Kindness of the Tlascalans—The soldiers of Narvaez murmur—Cortes receives unexpected reinforcements—The murmurers are sent home—He despatches messengers to Spain, Hispaniola, and Jamaica—Orders ship-timbers to be cut in the Tlascalan forests—Makes his head-quarters at Tezcuco—Death of Cuitlahuitzin—Guatimozin is made King of Mexico—Cortes attacks the cities Iztapalapan, Chalco, and Tlalmamalco—Sandoval reduces Zoltepec—The timbers for the brigantines are brought to Tezcuco—Xaltocan and Tacuba are reduced—Guatimozin refuses terms of peace—Quauhnahuac and Xochimilco are attacked—Narrow escape of Cortes—Conspiracy of Villafana—Courage and address of Cortes—The brigantines are launched . . . 140

CHAPTER IX.

The siege of Mexico is commenced—Dreadful massacre of the Spaniards on the causeways—Narrow escape of Cortes—Frightful festival of the Mexicans in the temple—Their cunning—Prudence of Cortes—The siege is renewed—Message to Guatimozin—His scornful answer—The Spaniards enter the capital—The last quarter is besieged—Guatimozin is made prisoner—The capital reduced—Disappointed avarice of the Spaniards—Guatimozin is put to the torture—Cortes snatches him from his tormentors—Death of the Mexican King—Conquest of the distant provinces—Enmity of the Bishop of Burgos toward Cortes—Rebuilding of the capital—Cortes liberates Narvaez 157

CHAPTER X.

Revolt in Panuco—Intrigues in Spain against Cortes—His friends support him—The King makes him Captain-General and Governor of New Spain—His great popularity—Arrival of Garay—Imprudence of his men—Slaughter of the Panuchese—The Bishop of Burgos and Narvaez continue their intrigues—Treachery and death of Christoval de Olid—March of Cortes to Honduras—The King issues a commission to investigate his conduct—Fidelity of the soldiers of Cortes—He embarks for Spain—Death of Sandoval—Reception of Cortes at the Spanish court—He returns to Mexico disappointed—Difficulties with the Audiencia—Embarks in new adventures—Discovery of California—Fails in his plans—Returns to Spain—Ingratitude of the King—Scornful treatment of the ministers—Death of Cortes—His remains are taken to Mexico 174

THE ADVENTURES OF HERNAN CORTES.

CHAPTER I.

WHO has not heard of that daring and fiery Spaniard, Hernan Cortes, the Conqueror of Mexico? The story of his exploits is as wild as a fable, and were it not now a well-known part of the history of Mexico, could scarcely be believed. To those of my young fellow-citizens who may be ignorant of his career, I offer the history of this remarkable man.

If you will look upon a map of Spain, in the province of Estremadura, you will find the small town of Medellin. At this place, in the year 1485, Hernan Cortes was born of poor but respectable parents. His parents (Don Martin Cortes de Monroy and Doña Catalina Pizarro de Altamirano) were of noble descent, had been once rich, but were now reduced. Whatever others may think, I consider it fortunate that young Cortes was born poor. Had he been the child of a rich man, he might have been reared in the midst of foolish luxuries and indulgences, led a life of idle dissipation, and proved utterly worthless: as it was, his poverty forced him to make exertions and to struggle with the world. Poverty helped him, as it has helped many others; it taught him to rely upon his own energies. It was particularly fortunate in his case; for his natural temperament, as you will see, was just such as to ruin him, had he been born to a rich inheritance.

Of the earliest years of his boyhood I can tell you nothing, except that he was a warm-hearted, sprightly, and intelligent lad, admired and beloved by all who knew him. At the age of fourteen he gave such promise of future usefulness, that his father determined he should have the advantage of an education, to fit him for the study of the law. Young Cortes was sent, therefore, at this time, to the celebrated University of Salamanca. Here, for the first time, he disappointed the expectations of his friends. His ardent and restless nature could not well bear the close industry and confinement of college life, and boys of inferior parts outstripped him in his studies. At the end of two years, I am sorry to say that he was worse than lazy. He was now so weary of his situation, that he became the leader of many wild and mischievous irregularities—so much so, that more than once he came near being expelled from the University. At length, to the great sorrow of his father, he left Salamanca, and returned to Medellin. Here, laying aside all books, he devoted himself to active and manly sports, and made himself skilful in horsemanship and the use of arms.

For some time he continued in this career, and being, unfortunately as it proved at the time, a boy of fine appearance, amiable disposition, and engaging manners, he brought about him many companions, and launched with them into many dissipations. His father was now very miserable. Far from dreaming that his son would ever reach honor or distinction, he feared that he was in a fair way to prove a worthless and unhappy man. One hope, however, was still left him. The boy had a passion for military life, and sighed for daring adventures as a soldier. This passion was carefully cultivated by the father, and in a little time, when an occasion presented itself, young Cortes showed that he was fully alive to it. The " Great Captain" Gonzalo de Cordova was adding to his fame in the wars in Italy, and crowds of Spanish youth were eager to flock to his standard. Among the rest was Hernan Cortes. Numbers enlisted, but when they were about starting on their march to join Cordova at Naples, young Cortes was suddenly seized with sickness, and thereby kept at home. This was a sad disappointment to the boy, as well as his father.

Another opportunity for adventure, however, soon offered, with fairer prospects for Cortes. Don Nicolas de Ovando, his kinsman, had been appointed the Governor of Hispaniola, and Don Martin supposed that, under the patronage of this kinsman, a fair field was opened before his son in the New World. Young Cortes now forgot his disappointment, and set his heart upon accompanying Don Nicolas. Great preparations were making for transporting the new Governor to his dominions; and, as he watched the progress, his desires were the more inflamed. Thirty-two ships were soon ready, and twenty-five hundred persons (many of them people of rank) were about embarking as settlers for the new colony. But when all was ready, Cortes was again prevented from being one of the number. This disappointment was brought about by his own folly and rashness. It seems that he had formed an attachment for a lady at Medellin, and on a dark night, before the ships set sail, was trying to reach the window of her chamber. In doing this, he had to scramble over an old wall, which unfortunately gave way under him, and he was severely injured by the fall.

The ships, therefore, sailed without him, leaving young Cortes sick and sorrowful, and his father deeply mortified.

At length, having slowly recovered, his father once more turned his thoughts toward the New World. Young Cortes still burned with the desire to join his kinsman Don Nicolas; and all being made ready accordingly, he left Medellin, and arrived safely at Saint Domingo, in the year 1504. Ovando welcomed him cordially, receiving him like his own son. He at once fixed him in places of distinction and profit, and seemed in every way determined to push his fortunes. Notwithstanding this, Cortes was restless, and in a little time panting for a wider field, where he might earn, as he thought, fame and glory. He was better satisfied when a circumstance occurred, which he thought opened that field. Two Spaniards, Ojeda and Nicuesa, had determined upon an expedition for the purpose of making discoveries and settlements upon the main land of America. Cortes heartily joined them in this enterprise, laboring with diligence to make all things ready. But when, at length, all was ready, his companions departed, leaving him too sick to undertake the voyage. He was now very miserable over this third disappointment, but afterwards, when he learned the result of that expedition, he looked upon the disappointment as a blessing. It was the most unfortunate attempt ever made by the Spaniards in the New World. The poor adventurers suffered sorely by tempests; and when at length they landed, the poisoned arrows of the natives, together with disease and famine, swept off the most of them. A little colony planted upon the Isthmus of Darien, by Vasco Nuñez de Balboa, was all that remained of the enterprise. Yet with all this, he had a thought that had he been among the adventurers, things might have gone better; and his heart was still bent upon discoveries and conquests. Among all the wild schemes of adventure talked of among the settlers at Hispaniola, none were too wild for him : he was ready, in fact, for any daring expedition,—the more daring the better.

In 1511, Don Diego Columbus, who had succeeded Ovando as Governor, determined upon the conquest of the island of Cuba, and Cortes resolved to bear his part in it. The Governor selected as the leader of this enterprise Diego Velasquez, a man well known in Hispaniola; and Cortes managed by his ability to be made, with Andres de Duero, joint secretary to Velasquez. In a little time all was ready, and Velasquez departed with a large number of followers. He anticipated a struggle in subduing the natives of the island, and had made preparations for it; but, strange to tell, an island seven hundred miles long, and covered with numerous inhabitants, was brought into subjection almost without an effort. The cacique Hatuey opposed his landing, and afterwards gave him some trouble, but with his three hundred men he was soon master of the island, and established several colonies, the principal one being at St. Jago.

Cortes, seeing the advantage of his position, cultivated warmly the friendship of Velasquez; and as he knew that Andres de Duero had his particular confidence, he managed to make a warm friend of him. Many of the people, however, soon became dissatisfied with Velasquez, and determined to send complaints against him to Don Diego Columbus. Cortes, by his manly bearing, had made friends of the multitude, and when they came to choosing some one who should bear their complaints, the boldness and sagacity of Cortes prompted them to choose him. It was a dangerous business, for the bearer would not only provoke Velasquez, but would risk his life in passing over to Hispaniola in a canoe. Yet Cortes imprudently agreed to undertake it. Velasquez was so provoked, that he declared he should suffer the punishment of death. Men were immediately ordered to arrest him. But Cortes, hearing of this, managed to make his escape, and hid himself in the church. Feeling safe here, he determined to remain until Andres de Duero could induce the commander to pardon him. His ardor and imprudence, however, soon revealed his hiding-place. He had formed an attachment for a young woman of good family, called Doña Catalina Suarez de Pacheco. She lived not far from the church, and Cortes was in the habit of meeting her. The officers knew this, and kept watch for him. One night, having left the church, thinking he was unseen, he was suddenly surprised, seized before he could make any resistance, and led off to prison. He seemed now to have so much sorrow for his error, that Velasquez was induced to forgive him. Afterwards, having married Doña Catalina, upon the birth of his first son, he requested the Governor to stand as the god-father. To this Velasquez cheerfully consented, and now they seemed as warm friends as ever. Cortes bore himself in every way kindly towards him, and lost no opportunity of making himself agreeable to him.

Desirous of extending his dominions, Velasquez, in the year 1517, had allowed Hernandez de Cordova to sail with a small expedition from Cuba, and he had discovered the eastern cape of Yucatan. It was an unfortunate expedition,—the commander and the greater portion of his soldiers having perished in it. Yet the accounts which Velasquez had received, induced him to fit out another and more powerful expedition. Four vessels were at once made ready, and Juan de Grijalva, at the head of two hundred and fifty men, took the command of them. In a short time, he discovered the island of Cozumel, and then following in the track of Cordova, coasted along the shores of Yucatan, trading with the natives, giving them such trinkets as he had, for gold and food. At last he made a landing on the island of St. Juan de Ulua. The Mexicans upon the coasts were now greatly alarmed. They had never seen such men or weapons as they now beheld, and they instantly sent messengers to their chief, Montezuma, telling him of the arrival of these new visiters. Montezuma was greatly frightened by their news. It is said that from this time he had no peace, living daily in the fear that his empire would be taken from him. The Spaniards remained several days at the island, and succeeded in finding some gold. Grijalva, after making his observations, became convinced that the coast near by was part of a continent, and he panted to land there and push his discoveries. There was danger, however, in this, as he did not know the character of the people whom he should meet, and the number of his men had been greatly reduced by disease. He resolved, therefore, to wait until he could get a reinforcement from Cuba, and accordingly sent a messenger back to Velasquez to get assistance. Having done this, he pursued his discoveries about the province of Panuco, which he found covered (it is said) with large and populous towns at the distance of three leagues from the coast.

In the mean time, his messenger, Pedro de Alvarado, had arrived in Cuba, bearing specimens of gold, and telling of the wonderful discoveries of Grijalva. Velasquez was greatly delighted: like all his countrymen at that time, he was thirsting for gold and conquests. His delight, too, was the greater, because he had heard nothing before from Grijalva since he sailed, and had feared he was lost. His fears had at one time been so intense, that he had despatched a vessel under the command of Christoval de Olid to seek him. Olid had followed in the track of his companions, but after being beaten about with tempests, had returned to Cuba without any tidings of them.

Alvarado's story soon spread over the island, and multitudes were eager to join Grijalva. The prospect of wealth and glory was now fairly opened before them, but among them all there was none more excited than Hernan Cortes. Velasquez immediately sent messengers to Spain with the glorious news of Grijalva's discovery, and then commenced fitting out an expedition for the new continent. The vessel was soon ready, and three hundred volunteers came forward, desirous of embarking. Among these were Diego de Ordaz, Francisco de Morla, Escobar, and Bernal Diaz del Castillo, who afterwards wrote a History of the

Conquest of Mexico. Now came the time for choosing a leader for this expedition. Velasquez knew very well that a good leader was everything in such an enterprise, and he was very cautious. Some recommended to the Governor to appoint Vasco Porcallo, a man of high rank, while the soldiers were in favor of Grijalva. Others spoke of Augustin Bermudez, and Bernardino Velasquez, relatives of the Governor, as fit persons, but none of them pleased Velasquez. The truth is, the Governor was jealous. He was desirous of appointing some one who was capable of leading the enterprise, and at the same time one who would not slight his authority. He was seeking his own glory.

From the beginning of the preparations, Hernan Cortes had determined, if possible, to be the leader of this expedition. He was himself on good terms with Velasquez, but was not willing to trust the chance of success to that. He knew that there were two individuals possessing more influence over the Governor than any others : these were Amador de Lares, the royal treasurer of Cuba, and Andres de Duero, his secretary ; and these, fortunately, were warm friends of his own. He bargained with these, therefore, to procure for him the command of the expedition, promising to reward them amply if they should succeed. Their attachment for Cortes, together with this hope of reward, induced them to urge his claim warmly. They declared to Velasquez that Cortes (as he well knew) was in every way fitted to take the command—that he was honorable, prudent, and fearless, and greatly beloved by all the Spaniards. Velasquez was pleased with the thought. He felt that Cortes was the proper man as to ability, and the thought that he possessed neither rank nor fortune, prevented any jealousy towards him. Cortes had behaved well whenever he had been trusted, and Velasquez was convinced he might be trusted now. Then, too, he remembered the friendship that had been kept between them since the marriage of Cortes, and naturally enough supposed that their former difficulty made him the safer man for this occasion. To the great joy of Cortes, Velasquez declared publicly that he was to be the leader of the expedition.

As soon as this appointment was made known, the disappointed relatives of the Governor began to beset him with strange stories of Cortes, hoping to startle his fears, that he might take the command from him. Nor did they work in vain. They succeeded so far in making him jealous, that his friends Lares and Duero became alarmed. They immediately gave notice to Cortes of what was doing, and he as quickly, before the poison had time fully to work, made all things ready for a start. He then went to see the Governor, and had a long talk with him about the whole enterprise. Velasquez was now so much pleased, that on the next morning, when Cortes was about to sail, he went with him to the vessel, and they had a warm and affectionate parting.

It was on the 18th day of November, 1519, that Cortes set sail from St. Jago. In a little time he reached Trinidad, a small settlement upon the island, and here discovered that his enemies were still at work to ruin him. Disappointed ambition s a base enemy to deal with. Cortes had no sooner sailed, than the kinsmen of the Governor told worse stories than ever. They knew the jealous nature of Velasquez, and worked upon it freely. They declared that Cortes was selfish and ambitious, and would despise his authority;—that he must expect nothing but insolence from him. Velasquez for some time felt easy; for notwithstanding his friendly parting with Cortes, he had given commands to Diego de Ordaz, one of the adventurers, to watch him, and report to him whatever was done. He felt, therefore, that he had a spy upon the actions of the leader, and this gave him confidence. But these disappointed men worked upon him until he began to feel that his spy would prove faithless. Then they began to frighten him in a new way: they hired a man named Juan Millian, who pretended to be an astrologer, to help them in their mean design, and this fellow prophesied terrible sorrows if the command was not taken from Cortes. All the suspicions of Velasquez were now roused. He knew the vessel was to touch at Trinidad, and now he sent his messengers with positive orders to Francisco Verdugo, the chief magistrate of the place. These orders were, to take the command from Cortes and give it to Vasco Porcallo. Secret instructions were sent also to Diego de Ordaz to assist in this matter. But, fortunately, the friends of Cortes had not forgotten him. Lares and Duero knew what mischief was at work, and they secretly sent news of the whole to Cortes. He at once understood the danger of his position, and understood as well how to meet it. Knowing that much depended upon making a friend of Diego de Ordaz, he sought him immediately. The open bearing of Cortes, with his powerful persuasions and brilliant promises, at once won the friendship of Ordaz. So far from aiding the commands given to Verdugo, he went to the magistrate and convinced him that it was impossible to obey the commands of Velasquez. Cortes, he declared, had the hearts of the people, and it was idle to oppose him. Some think that Verdugo was bribed, but it is more probable that the great popularity of Cortes made him afraid to attempt to carry out his orders. At all events, Cortes was undisturbed. To blind Velasquez, he now wrote him a friendly letter, and then set sail from Trinidad

Ere long he reached Havana, another settlement. Here he commenced beating up recruits, and gathering stores and provisions to strengthen his armament. This was easily done; multitudes eagerly joined him. Cortes hurried this business as rapidly as possible, for he still feared the jealousy of the suspicious Governor, and expected every hour the arrival of orders to stop him. In this fear he was not mistaken. He had not yet completed his arrangements, when the order came. Velasquez, more enraged against him than ever, because Verdugo had not obeyed his commands, and now certain that Cortes meant to defy him, sent a messenger with secret instructions to Pedro Barba, the commander at Havana, ordering him at once to seize Cortes, send him under a strong guard to St. Jago, and then delay the expedition until he should receive further orders. The principal officers were also commanded to aid Pedro Barba in arresting Cortes. Fortunately for Cortes, he was again advised of this plan. Bartholomew de Olmedo, chaplain to his armament, having received from a monk secret information of the whole, informed Cortes, and he at once prepared to meet the danger. The two officers whom he most feared as being ready to assist Pedro Barba, were Velasquez de Leon, a relation of the Governor of Cuba, and Diego de Ordaz, whose conduct, notwithstanding what had passed at Trinidad, was sometimes suspicious.

Velasquez de Leon was a frank, warm-hearted, and ambitious young man, and Cortes easily won him to his cause by telling him of the glory that was before him, and the danger of any delay to the expedition. As to Ordaz, he determined to get him out of the way for a time, and therefore sent him to Guaniguanico, near Cape Antonio, that he might get further supplies of provisions for the voyage. As soon as Ordaz had left, Cortes assembled all his men. He now told them of the meanness and jealousy of Velasquez, in trying to take the command from him for no cause whatever. Then he spoke of the foolish order for delaying an expedition in which they were all so eager to embark, and in which they were all to earn so much glory, —an order he declared to be the more outrageous, because they had all spent their own private means in equipping for the enterprise. The men were greatly aroused. They were attached to Cortes, and they knew his worth as their leader. They begged that he would never give up the command, and promised that they would risk their lives anywhere, wherever he might lead. This was precisely what Cortes desired. He declared that he would be their leader, and that he would guide them to that rich and beautiful country for which they were panting—a country in which every man should find wealth and honor. He then took an oath that he would never forsake such faithful and trusty followers. The air now rang with their shouts. While some cried out that they would stand by Cortes for ever, others uttered terrible threats against his enemies. He was now fixed in his command; he had the hearts of all his men. They looked upon him as a leader chosen by themselves—their noble and bold friend and companion, who was to lead them on to victory. Pedro Barba at once wrote to Velasquez, telling him that it was impossible to fulfil his orders; and Cortes sent him a second letter, informing him that on the next day he should sail from Havana.

The fleet of Cortes now consisted of eleven vessels, one of which was of one hundred tons, three of seventy, and the rest only open barks. His followers numbered six hundred and seventeen persons. Of these, one hundred and nine were sailors and mechanics; the remainder were to act as soldiers. As to regular soldiers, there were among them all, only sixteen horsemen, thirty musketeers, and thirty-two cross-bowmen; the others were armed only with spears and swords, the use of which they little understood. To add somewhat to their strength, however, there were on board the fleet " ten cannons and four falconets." Instead of shields or coats of mail to defend them from such enemies as they should meet, which articles would have proved heavy in a warm climate, their leader had supplied them all with jackets quilted with cotton. This was the whole force, with which Cortes was now prepared to seek and subdue the new continent.

To urge his followers onward the more, Cortes mingled with their dreams of glory, the thought that they were to extend the religion of our blessed Saviour. The spirit of the age, and the religion in which they had been trained, allowed this idea, and they really supposed that their warlike expedition, among other things, was to spread the gospel of peace. Strange thought, yet it was theirs! The Spaniards therefore hailed with enthusiasm the banner which Cortes raised over them. It was a standard of velvet, richly embroidered with gold, bearing the royal arms and a large cross, together with this motto: *" Companions, let us follow the cross, for under this guidance we shall conquer."*

CHAPTER II.

CORTES having divided his men into eleven companies, and placed captains over them,* they all embarked, and on the 10th of February set sail from Havana. Ere long they came near the island Cozumel. The frightened inhabitants, seeing the approach of the fleet, fled from the shores. Nor were they idly frightened, for they soon felt the hands of the plunderers. Pedro de Alvarado's company was the first to land, and seeing in one of the temples an idol, beautifully adorned with gold, they instantly stripped it, and seized two or three of the natives Cortes, seeing that such rashness would at once ruin

---

* The names of these captains, many of whom were afterwards distinguished, were as follows: Juan Velasquez de Leon, Pedro de Alvarado, Hernandez Portocarrero, Francisco de Montejo, Christoval de Olid, Juan de Escalante, Francisco de Morla, Francisco Salcedo, Juan Escobar, and Gnies Gnortes. Cortes himself had charge of one of the companies.

his prospects, immediately rebuked Alvarado, and caused him to release the prisoners and deliver up the ornaments. Upon this the natives lost some of their fears, and mingled freely with the new-comers.

Cortes now observed that the natives frequently used the word *Castillano*, and this led to an important discovery. He knew that the word must have been learned of some Spaniard, and therefore supposed that one or more of his countryme might be on the island. After a long search, he succeeded in finding one man, and the poor fellow was happy indeed when they discovered him, for he had gone through many sorrows. He was completely black, was covered only with a few rags thrown loosely over his shoulders and around his waist, and had grown to be, in his manners, almost an Indian. Upon his back he carried a small bundle, in which, among other trifles that he had, were some pieces of a prayer-book. It was with great difficulty that he told his story to his countrymen, for he had almost lost the use of his native tongue. His name (he said) was Geronimo de Aguilar. He was a native of Ecija, and had received holy orders. Eight years before, he had been wrecked on a voyage from Darien to Hispaniola. He and his companions tried to save themselves in a boat, but storms had driven them upon the coast of Cozumel, where they were seized by the natives and

luced to slavery. Some of them had at length
en sacrificed, and many had died of hard labor.
 had at last, by the providence of God, found a
end in one of the Caciques, who took care of
n and treated him with kindness. Of all his
npanions, one only remained beside himself,
1 he had joined the Indians and become one of
eir tribe. Cortes immediately took this poor
low into his service, and, as it turned out, he
)ved a great help in acting as an interpreter be-
een his countrymen and the Indians.
On the fourth of March the fleet left Cozumel
1 moved towards the river Tabasco. At this
ice Cortes expected a friendly meeting with the
tives, inasmuch as Grijalva had there been treat-
 very kindly. In this he was disappointed. It
ems that these friendly people had been reproach-
 by the neighboring tribes, for their kind recep-
n of Grijalva. And now, when Cortes came in
ht, instead of friends he found enemies. Every
ng seemed warlike. He saw canoes moving
out filled with warriors, and thousands of men
sembled on the shore to oppose him. Cortes at
ce knew that he was to have a struggle, but, de-
ous of peace if possible, he requested of the peo-
 through Aguilar, that he might meet their chiefs.
iis they promptly refused, at the same time ma-
ig dreadful threats against the Spaniards. Cor-
; made no farther attempt to treat with them, but

determined at once to disembark near the town, and meet the difficulty. Accordingly, he kept on his course up the river. The natives, seeing this movement, flocked to the spot where they supposed he would land. Crowds soon covered the banks of the river in that quarter, shouting and making a tremendous noise with their trumpets and drums. Nevertheless, the fleet cast anchor, and the landing commenced. Clouds of arrows were now poured in upon them from the land, while the warriors in their canoes opposed them fiercely with their lances. But the resolute Spaniards were not to be driven back. Through the water and mud, they fought their way in spite of numbers, and reached the bank. This was no sooner done, than Cortes placed himself at the head of his men, and made a tremendous attack upon the natives, which soon scattered them. He now reviewed his troops, and found that fourteen of his followers had been wounded. He resolved, therefore, not to pursue the enemy, but fixed his camp for the night, and posted his sentinels around to prevent any surprise.

In the mean time, the news of their defeat was carried through the country by the Indians, and they rallied in strong numbers for another struggle upon the great plain of Ceutla. Cortes had expected this, and prepared himself to meet it. His horses (thirteen only in number) were brought ashore, the best riders were mounted upon them, and he himself took the command of this little troop of cavalry. His other troops (the infantry and artillery) were trusted to the command of Ordaz and Mesa. Matters being thus arranged, he pushed forward to meet the enemy. Ere long, they came in sight of them. The whole plain was covered with the multitude, and a hideous looking multitude it was. With their faces daubed with red and black paint, and armed with their shields, lances, bows, and slings, they were moving about, making ready for the battle; while here and there the Spaniards marked the chiefs, with tufts of feathers on their heads, who seemed to be urging them on. The woods rang with the noise of their drums and trumpets. Sweeping round the plain with his horsemen, Cortes managed to pass unseen to the rear of the enemy, so as to prevent any retreat, while his other troops were to move directly forward and attack them in front. The Indians, however, did not wait for their attack. Thinking the first blow the best, they gave it themselves. As soon as they saw them, they pressed forward and let fly a tremendous volley of arrows. The Spaniards for a moment fell back; one man was killed, and twenty wounded. The artillery troops now rushed forward, and bringing their guns to bear, literally raked down the Indians. Notwithstanding this, the Indians waged the fight furiously and fearlessly, and the chances of war were in their favor, until Cortes showed himself. The plain was smooth, and he with his horsemen swept over it, carrying everything before them. This decided the day. The frightened Indians now saw that resistance was idle; they looked upon horse and rider as one tremendous monster; and such as could, fled for the woods and marshes. Eight hundred of their number were left dead on the field, while two Spaniards only had been killed.

This was their second defeat, and now they were ready to submit. Fifteen men, with their faces painted black in sign of sorrow, were soon sent to the Spanish camp, bearing presents of fowls, corn, and roasted fish. Cortes received them with so much kindness, that on the next day thirty of the chief warriors came forward and begged the privilege of burying their dead. This favor Cortes readily granted. He feared, however, that these people were treacherous, and in a little time might rally again to oppose him. As soon, therefore, as the melancholy duty of burying the dead was ended, he assembled the people before him, and threatened awful vengeance if they attempted any further opposition. To frighten them the more, he caused one of the cannons to be discharged, and then his best-trained horses and riders were brought out, and various terrifying feats performed before them. The frightened natives now looked upon the Spaniards with amazement and reverence, and at once promised fidelity to the Spanish king. Not satisfied with professions of love, they brought to Cortes many strange presents, such as toys of gold, made to look like dogs, lizards, ducks, and other animals; and to prove their friendship with a crowning gift, they presented to him twenty of their women.

This last was the most valuable present, for among these women there was one who afterwards became known under the name of Doña Marina, and proved a great help to Cortes. She was a female of high rank among her countrymen—the daughter of a cacique or prince, who held his dominions subject to the Emperor of Mexico. Unhappily for her, her father died while she was an infant. Her mother afterwards married again, and having a son by her new husband, learned to despise her daughter. Her feelings were so bitter towards the child, that she determined to cheat her of her inheritance, that she might gain it for the boy. Accordingly, she secretly gave her away to some merchants of Xicallanco, and at the same time spread the story far and wide that the child was dead. The merchants to whom she was given sold her to one of the chiefs of Tabasco, and the chief now presented her to Cortes. This woman, as you will see, proved of great service in two ways. First, she acted as an interpreter: understanding the Mexican language and the Maja tongue also, which Aguilar understood, she was able to interpret between the Spaniards and Mexicans. Then, too, she understood the manners, habits, and prejudices of the natives, and was enabled to help Cortes to many advantages, and to guard him against many dangers—all which she did cheerfully, for she soon formed a strong attachment for the Spanish leader.

Having thus brought the natives to his own terms, Cortes prepared to leave Tabasco. He caused his men (together with the Indians, who cheerfully assisted) to erect upon the plain of Ceutla a large cross made of the *Cieba*-tree, as a memorial of his victory; and then Palm Sunday being at hand, he brought all the natives of the neighborhood together to worship around the cross with Father Olmedo. The Spaniards say, that many of these poor men were at once made converts to Christianity, and baptized by Olmedo; but this can hardly be believed. Many were baptized, but probably not one of them knew what he was doing. They readily obeyed any wish of the Spaniards, and one wish was that they should be baptized. At all events, in the evening they parted good friends to their conquerors, the Indians promising a "perpetual love;" and the next morning the fleet set sail for the harbor of San Juan de Ulua.

Early in April,[*] they reached that harbor

[*] Robertson says, the beginning of April—Bernal Diaz says, the 21st.

Scarcely had they dropped their anchors and hoisted their standard, when Cortes saw two large canoes, full of people, coming towards the fleet. Two of these people seemed to be persons of note, and, without any signs of fear, came on board the principal vessel. They spoke to Cortes in a friendly way, and by means of Aguilar and Doña Marina, he was able to understand them. They were messengers (they said) from the chief who was trusted with the command of that province by the great Emperor Montezuma, and were sent to learn what had brought Cortes to their country, and also to offer any assistance they could render him for prosecuting his voyage. Cortes, in his turn, received them very kindly, assuring them that he himself was the subject of a mighty king, and had a message of great importance to deliver to their sovereign, which would greatly help their country; and that he had towards them no thoughts but those of peace and friendship. At his invitation, they then refreshed themselves by eating, and after this they were sent back to the chief, loaded with quantities of toys as presents. The chief and his people were now greatly delighted. Far from opposing his landing, they were ready to aid him in making it, and when he ordered his men to erect their huts upon the shore, in this also they cheerfully assisted. After a little time, a number came, bringing supplies of bread, fowls, and fruit, with a promise that the governor of the province would shortly visit him.

Accordingly, on the next day, their chief, whose name was Teutchlile, in company with Quitlalpitoc, another chief, came to the Spanish camp with a great train of followers. Cortes received them with great respect, and invited them to eat with him. This being over, he informed Teutchlile that he was a subject to Don Carlos, the greatest monarch of the world, and at his desire had come to their country with an important message to their sovereign; that the message was such a one that he could deliver it to no person expect the Emperor himself, and therefore hoped he might immediately be allowed to see him. This greatly startled the two chiefs. They knew the fears and apprehensions of Montezuma since the appearance of strangers upon the coast, and that it would be impossible to obtain the privilege which Cortes sought,—and yet they were afraid to rouse the Spaniard by a refusal. Hoping to satisfy him in another way, Teutchlile at once ordered certain rich presents to be brought forward, which he declared that Montezuma had sent, in the hope that Cortes would receive them. These consisted of a quantity of fine cotton garments, plumes of many different colors, and a variety of toys made of gold. The poor ignorant Indian did not know that the demand of Cortes was made only that he might reach the heart of their country, and that the sight of his rich presents would only excite him the more, and make him the more determined to carry out his purpose. Cortes received his presents in a friendly way, and in return gave them, as presents for Montezuma, some artificial diamonds, a richly-carved arm-chair, and a crimson cap adorned with a golden medal of Saint George; and, with this, demanded more earnestly that he might be taken to the Emperor to deliver his message.

While all this was going on, some of the followers of Teutchlile were busy in painting upon pieces of white cotton, pictures of the strangers, with their ships, horses, and cannon. Cortes, hearing that these pictures were to be taken to Montezuma, that he might learn something of his new visiters, determined that with them the painters should carry such a report as should terrify the Emperor. Accordingly, he immediately ordered his troops to form in battle array, and with great skill they went through their military exercises. Then his horsemen were brought forward, and the Mexicans stood speechless as they looked at their fierce and wonderful performances. Next the cannon were discharged, and now they were completely overcome: some fled, while others fell flat on their faces. It was with great difficulty that Cortes, after a while, succeeded in calming their fears, and bringing them all again around him.

Cortes now again urged his demand, and at length, with fair promises that his message and presents should be delivered to Montezuma, and that he should soon have an answer, Teutchlile with his train was leaving the camp, when suddenly he saw a helmet which he greatly desired. It looked (as he said) like the helmet that adorned the head of *Huitzilopochtli*, their god of war, and begged that he might present it to the Emperor. This request Cortes readily granted, and they all departed. This last gift, as you will see, proved to be a most unfortunate present.

Before these messages reached Montezuma, he had been greatly alarmed by rumors as to these strangers. It seems that the Mexican Empire was managed with great system in every way. Along the principal roads, couriers were placed at certain distances, and through them news was rapidly carried from one end to the other of the empire. In this way he had gathered strange stories of Cortes and his followers. At length the messengers arrived. Montezuma was pleased with the presents, but their pictures, together with their stories and the helmet, greatly increased his alarm. The helmet called up in his heart the saddest forebodings. His head was full of superstitions, and he saw in this helmet something which told him of the end of his empire. There was a strange tradition among the Mexicans at this time, "that *Quetzalcoatl*, the god of the air, had disappeared a long time ago, promising to return after a certain time to rule over the people of Mexico."* Montezuma fancied that these Spaniards in their armor were like the god of the air, and trembled for his authority. To the demand of Cortes he gave a positive refusal, and yet, afraid to provoke him, to lessen his disappointment, and secure his friendship, he determined upon sending him some very rich presents. Accordingly, in less than a week, Teutchlile and his followers again reached the Spanish camp, laden with these presents.

As they came into the presence of Cortes now, in token of respect they touched the earth with their fingers, and then kissed them. Their splendid presents were then brought forward. There were cloths of cotton worked so finely that they resembled silk, beautiful pictures made of different colored feathers, various toys of animals made of gold, together with collars and bracelets of the same precious metal, pearls and precious stones, and, best of all in the eyes of the Spaniards, was an enormous plate of gold made in the form of a circle, to represent the Mexican age of fifty years, having the sun in the centre.† Cortes received

---

* Clavigero's Mexico.
† This piece was very massive, nor could it be less than ten thousand sequins in real value.—Clavigero's Mexico.

these with great delight, and then demanded when he should see the Emperor. The messengers, in as mild a way as possible, informed him that Montezuma was not disposed to see him at his court; that he feared the Mexicans would be excited if strange soldiers were seen in the capital of the empire, and moreover that he thought it dangerous for Cortes to attempt to reach him, inasmuch as he would have to pass through barren deserts, meeting many hostile tribes. Cortes was now more decided than ever. He insisted upon being taken immediately to the emperor, declaring that he would never leave their country, until he had faithfully delivered the message of his master Don Carlos.

The messengers were now in a worse condition than before. They had seen Montezuma's fears, and they now saw Cortes' resolution. Afraid to offend either party, they at last prevailed upon Cortes to remain with his men where he was, until they should bring him a farther message from Montezuma.

Reaching the capital again, they found the Emperor in the same fearful state of mind, and his fears became greater when he learned how Cortes persisted in his demand. It seems strange, that this great monarch should have been so much startled by the appearance of a handful of strangers in his kingdom. His dominions were two hundred

...agues from north to south, and five hundred from ...st to west; they were covered by a numerous ...d warlike race of men, and he himself had almost ...e complete control of his people. Often had he ...d them on to victory, until his name had come to ... a protection to friends and a terror to enemies, ...d had he at once marched against the Spaniards ... might readily have crushed them. But the truth ..., he was a slave to superstitious fears, and, like ...ost men frightened in this way, the longer he look-...l at danger, the greater it seemed to be. The poor ...an's head was filled with old traditions, and ...rophecies, and strange dreams, and everything ...eemed to tell him that the end of his great empire ...as at hand. When the messengers told him that ...ortes still insisted on seeing him, he was pro-...oked as well as frightened at his boldness. In a ...orm of passion, he swore that the Spaniards ...hould never leave his country; that he would ...eize them all, and sacrifice them to the gods—...en his fears mastered him, and he gave up all ...ought of attacking them. Thus wavering be-...ween anger and fear, he did not know what to ..., and was hardly fit to attempt anything. At ...ngth, he despatched his messengers, with posi-...ve orders to Cortes to leave his country imme-...iately, while at the same time his fears prompted ...im to load these same messengers, with rich pres-...nts once more for the Spanish chief.

CHAPTER III.

WHEN Teutchlile again reached the Spanish camp, Cortes was in the midst of difficulties with his own men. Notwithstanding his great popularity, it seems there were some few in his army who were friends to Velasquez, and these watched all his movements very closely. They had noticed that in all his orders, and especially in taking possession of the island Cozumel, the name of Velasquez was not even once mentioned, and they now began to beat up friends among the men, declaring that Cortes was selfishly ambitious, thinking only of himself, and seeking his own glory. Dissatisfied themselves, they magnified every little trouble, to make the men discontented also with their leader. The spot where the camp was pitched was sandy, and swarmed with musquitoes, and this was spoken of. The provisions were becoming scanty—the bread was spoiled—the bacon was rotting—and they alarmed the men with the fear of starvation. This scarcity of food Cortes had himself noticed, and had proposed to seize on the strong town of Chiahuitzla, where they would find supplies. This they complained of, saying that it was risking their lives for nothing, that they were but a small band, already weakened by disease and fatigue, and could hope for no success in such an undertaking. The spirit of discontent was thus beginning to run high, when the messenger arrived with positive orders from Montezuma that the strangers should leave his country. Cortes received this message with great calmness, and tried to frighten the messenger, but Teutchlile only treated him with scorn, and left the camp very angry.

Now the murmurs among the discontented became louder. They looked upon the message of Montezuma as a declaration of war against them, and openly declared they were not able to meet it. Diego de Ordaz, their principal leader, was chosen to go before Cortes in their name, to tell him of the madness of remaining in the country, and that they were determined to return to Cuba.

Cortes received this also with great coolness and at once ordered his troops to prepare for their return. But the truth is, that as these difficulties had been increasing, he had prepared himself to overcome them. He knew that he had certain strong friends around him. These were Portocarrero, Sandoval, Alvarado, Escalante, Olid, Lugo, and Bernal Diaz, and to these he had spoken plainly telling them of the danger that threatened the expedition, and they had spoken to many of the men. These now came forward and declared that they could never think of returning; that they had spent all their means, and left every comfort to embark in the enterprise, and that it was cruelty to them to turn back merely because some of the men were too cowardly to go on. They called on their commander to lead them on to victory, since they were ready to follow, and to let all who were not bold enough for the adventure, return to the Governor of Cuba. This was precisely what Cortes desired and expected. In reply, he declared that he was ready and anxious to remain, and had proposed a return homeward, only because he supposed it was the desire of his followers; that now he was delighted to find he had mistaken their wishes. Since they had shown the fearless feeling of true Spaniards, he was ready to lead them on, and should try to prove himself a proper commander for such brave adventurers. These words of Cortes had a wonderful effect upon the army.

Still his plan was not yet completed. As the friends of Velasquez thought that his authority was slighted, Cortes determined that he would make himself in every way independent of that authority. For this purpose, he now, with great solemnity, commenced a settlement in the country, giving to the new colony the name of Villa Rica de la Vera Cruz.* The men were all assembled next, to choose officers for the new colony; and, as Cortes expected, the authority was given to Portocarrero, Alvarado, and Olid, three of his principal friends. As soon as these officers met in council, he came before them. He began by telling them that they were intrusted with great powers for the good of the settlement, and that he should be always ready to support them; and that since they were the chosen officers of the people, he could not think it right or proper that he should any longer keep the command which was given to him by Velasquez. He had come, therefore, to deliver up his commission to them, and was ready to take his place in the army as a common soldier. With this he left them.

He had no sooner departed, than the three officers elected him to the command of the army, as well as to the chief management of the colony. Then, to secure the good feelings of the men, the whole army was at once assembled, and they told them what they had done. All the former success of Cortes was now set forth before them, together with his bravery and generosity, and the bright

* The rich town of the True Cross.

prospects before all those who should follow such a leader. The men were greatly excited. They vowed their attachment to Cortes, and took an oath to stand by him at all hazards. Some few still held back, but they were brought over by presents and promises. Now the ringleaders, Diego de Ordaz, Velasquez de Leon, Escobar, and Escudero, were more angry than ever, and spoke more loudly against Cortes, in spite of all the numbers in his favor. To stop this, he instantly caused these men to be seized and fastened with fetters. In a few days they were set free, and Cortes offered to send them back to Cuba; but they chose rather to remain with him now. Their discontent seemed at an end, and all was again quiet and peaceable. Thus Cortes had managed to be more firmly fixed than ever in the hearts of his companions. His difficulties had only aided him.

As they still felt the want of food, Alvarado was now sent with a hundred men to scour the neighboring country, and, if possible, obtain supplies. In a little time, he returned with good news, but he and his men had been startled by some things which they saw. They had passed through certain villages, where there was abundance of food, and in one had entered one of the temples of the natives. There, to their great horror, they found the bleeding bodies of men and boys who had just been sacrificed, for the knife lay reeking with blood beside them. It was impossible for him to learn anything from most of the natives whom he saw, for they fled at the sight of him. He had met only one party who seemed friendly, and these were laden with provisions, and seemed to be going towards the Spanish camp. In a short time, this party came in with their supplies, and presented themselves before Cortes as messengers from the Cacique of Chempoalla, with a warm invitation from the Cacique that the strangers would visit him.

Cortes received them kindly, but doubted at first as to accepting this invitation, fearing there was treachery in it. He asked the messengers many questions, and at length discovered that their Cacique, though subject to the Emperor of Mexico, was no friend to Montezuma. This was enough to bring him to a conclusion, for he at once saw what advantage he might make of it. He therefore dismissed them, thanking the Cacique for his kindness, and promising that he would soon come and see him.

The spot where the settlement was begun was not a good one, and Cortes only waited for the arrival of Francisco de Montejo, whom he had sent in search of a better, to keep his promise with the Chempoallans. At the end of twelve days he came back, reporting that he had found a place called Quiabislan, with a fine harbor and a fertile soil. Cortes determined at once to remove his settlement there, and as Chempoalla lay in the way to this place, he was soon ready for his departure. When the Spaniards reached Chempoalla, they were surprised and pleased to see its large houses and wide streets lined with beautiful trees. The meeting was very friendly between the Cacique and the Spanish chief. The Cacique came forward with his principal men, all dressed in rich mantles of fine cotton, adorned with gold, and Cortes at once embraced him. He immediately began to complain of the cruelty and oppression of Montezuma, and expressed great joy that the Spaniards had arrived. Cortes at once saw that the poor man deserved and needed protection, and therefore, weak as he was with his little band, he offered himself as his protector. It was the desire of the Emperor Don Carlos whom he served (he said), that he should protect the weak, and free all who were oppressed; that he saw that his wrongs were many under the cruel tyrant Montezuma, and in a little time he would see that they were ended. With this promise he left the Chempoallans greatly delighted, and pushed on to Quiabislan.

He found this place to be just what Montejo had described it, and immediately marked out the ground for making the settlement. Then he led the way in the work, carrying materials and digging the ground for the foundation. His officers them in the midst of the temple. The next command was to wash and purify the place; and after this the holy cross was raised upon the altar, and Father Olmedo invited the people to worship. The poor Chempoallans submitted to this, for they were weak and needed his protection.

The followers of Cortes had now been in the country nearly three months, and began to grow impatient to march toward Mexico. He was himself as eager as any, but had not yet arranged all things as he desired. The thought of the opposition of Velasquez tormented him, and he was determined if possible to have the approbation of Don Carlos, the King of Spain. He gathered his principal friends together, and told them that before starting, he thought it best to send special messengers to the King; and that, to please Don Carlos, it would be well to send to him by the same messengers a present of all the treasures thus far discovered. These friends approved the plan, and proposed it to the men. Strange to tell, almost every man willingly stripped himself of all he had gained thus far to swell the present of Don Carlos. It was for the common good, and that was sufficient. Portocarrero and Montejo were at once chosen as the messengers. With positive instructions that they should by no means touch in their voyage to Spain at the Island of Cuba, the messengers set sail, bearing to Don Carlos the present and a letter from the officers of Villa Rica, giving glorious accounts of Cortes, and the rich country which he had discovered for the kingdom of Spain.

The messengers had scarcely left, when a plot was formed by some of the soldiers and sailors to seize one of the vessels, sail to Cuba, and inform Velasquez of what was going on, that he might stop them on their way. The plot was so secretly managed, that it was discovered just in time to prevent it. The conspirators had gone on board the vessel, when one of their number, named Coria, who was about joining them, suddenly repented of his treachery, came to Cortes, and informed him of the plan. He immediately went on board the vessel, and not one of them dared deny the crime. They were all seized and brought ashore. Escudero and Centeno, the ringleaders, were instantly put to death; Umbria, the pilot, had one of his feet cut off; and two of the sailors received two hundred lashes. This was terrible punishment, but Cortes excused himself by the plea of necessity. The rest of the gang he spared, saying that they were unfortunately led off by the bad example of the ringleaders.

Cortes was now very unhappy. This plot convinced him that there were still dissatisfied men in his camp; that all was not peace as he supposed. He knew that where this was the case, troubles

the same kind were likely to occur again; but
his anxiety a thought flashed upon his mind,
at he would prevent them for ever. A bold
termination was now in his heart. He again
thered his principal friends, and told them that
was resolved to destroy the fleet; that thereby
would gain all the sailors for soldiers; and that
s men, having then no chance of escape, must
ther conquer or die. As usual, they approved
his daring resolution; the soldiers were talked
, and many were ready to join heart and hand in
plan which added one hundred sailors to the
my. Escalante was soon busy in dismantling
e ships, and the hulls were sunk. The skiffs
ly were saved, for the purpose of fishing. Thus
ey were locked up in the country. To conquer
die was truly all that was now before them, and
ortes at once commenced his preparations for
vading Mexico.

Assembling all his men at Chempoalla, he made
stirring speech to his army, telling them of the
ory that was before them. The force now con-
sted of five hundred infantry, fifteen horsemen,
d six pieces of cannon. To these he added two
indred Indians of a low grade, called *Tamenes*,
ho were to act as beasts of burden, and four hun-
ed warriors, selected, by the request of the Ca-
que of Chempoalla, from among his troops.
hen taking from the Caciques a promise that they

would aid, as far as they could, his settlement at Villa Rica, left under the command of Escalante, he was ready for the march.

At this moment, a messenger came in hot haste from Villa Rica, to tell him that a vessel was cruising near the coast. This startled Cortes; in an instant he supposed that this was some ship sent against him by Velasquez. Leaving the command of the army to Alvarado and Sandoval, he immediately set off, with a small party of horse, for Villa Rica. As he came near, he marked the vessel at some distance from the shore, and presently saw in his way four strange Spaniards coming towards him. It seems that these men were a part of the crew of the strange vessel, and had been sent to the shore by the captain, Alonso de Pineda, to take possession of the country. The captain was aware that Cortes was in possession, and had given them a document to present to him,—which document stated that, by a royal commission, Francisco de Garay, the Governor of Jamaica, was to have authority over all the coast he might discover to the north of the river of Saint Peter and Saint Paul. Three ships had therefore been sent by Garay, bringing two hundred and seventy soldiers, under the command of Pineda, who was just now in the river of Panuco. They presented the document, at the same time commanding Cortes not to come upon the new territory of Garay. Receiving it, he begged that he might see their captain, and make a fair arrangement with him, declaring that they were both subjects to Don Carlos, and seeking the glory of their common kingdom. This they refused ; and Cortes, without hesitation, ordered them to be seized. He then hid himself with his men all night behind a sand-hill near the coast, hoping that more soldiers would be sent from the ships to look for their comrades, and that he might seize them and persuade them to join him. Finding himself disappointed in this, he now employed a stratagem to bring them ashore. Four of his men were dressed in the prisoners' clothes, and sent to the coast to make signals. In a little time, a boat was seen making to the shore. From some cause or other (suspicion of the plot, perhaps), only three men landed—the rest pushing off, and hurrying back to the ship. These three, however, were instantly secured. Having now no hope of gaining more men, and little to fear, as he thought, from Francisco de Garay, with his seven new soldiers he pushed back to his army.

On the 16th of August, the army commenced the march towards Mexico. For a little time they fared very well, passing through Xalapan, Socochima, and Texotla, where the people were independent of Montezuma, and consequently received them very kindly. After this they came upon a wild and mountainous region, filled ith frightful precipices, where no human being lived. The weather was extremely cold, provisions began to run low, and withal they were pelted by heavy hail-storms. They felt now that their hardships had commenced; but, trained to difficulties, and thirsting for glory, they moved on without a murmur. At length they arrived at Xocotlan, on the confines of Mexico, and were greatly cheered by the change. The chief city lay in a beautiful valley at the foot of the mountains; the lofty temples, and houses plastered and whitewashed, rose pleasantly before them, and for a moment they thought of their homes in the Old World. Cortes at once sent a message to the Cacique, informing him of his arrival; and he presently showed himself, with a large number of followers. The Spanish chief was greeted kindly, to all appearance, but, as he thought, not sincerely; and he was confirmed in this thought when he found that his troops were but poorly provided for. He considered it best, however, to make no complaints. For five days he remained at this place, learning all that he could of Montezuma and his kingdom. He questioned the Cacique very closely, and was told in reply that Montezuma was the most powerful and wealthy monarch in the world; and while he richly rewarded all his friends, his enemies were always looked upon as wretched beings, and sacrificed to the gods. The city of Mexico, where he dwelt, was a strong fortress, where no enemy could take him. It was built in a lake, and could only be reached by three causeways, each of which had several chasms, which could only be passed by means of wooden bridges. The Spaniards heard all this with perfect calmness, and the Xocotlans began to look upon them also as *Teules*, or deities. The thought that men could live without fearing the great Montezuma, was to them incredible. Then the skill of the soldiers, together with the appearance of the cannons and horses, startled the Cacique the more, and he now showed a disposition to be very friendly.

When Cortes was leaving, he seemed greatly interested in him, and urged him, on his journey to Mexico, to take the route through the province of Cholula. There were multitudes of people (he said) in that province, for the most part peaceable men, living by cultivating the soil: there the Spaniards would meet with a kind reception, and find abundance. The Chempoallans, however, were of a different opinion. They now came forward, stating that the Cholulans were a treacherous race; that no man could put any confidence in them; and besides this, that their chief city was guarded by a garrison of Mexican soldiers. They begged that he would make his journey through the province of Tlascala, where the people were fierce and warlike, hated Montezuma, and would gladly receive him; moreover, that these Tlascalans were strong friends to them and the Totonacas. Cortes, thinking the advice of old friends, of whom he had had some trial, better than that of new ones, determined to go by the way of Tlascala.

CHAPTER IV.

RENEWING his march, in a little time Cortes reached Xalacingo, on the borders of the Tlascalan dominions, and immediately prepared to send messengers into their country, to tell them of his arrival. Four Chempoallans of high rank were chosen for this purpose. Dressed after the manner of ambassadors (with cotton mantles full of knots at the ends), and bearing a long arrow tipped with white feathers, the symbol of peace,* they departed. Contrary to all expectation, they were received unkindly. The Tlascalans at once seized them, and prepared to sacrifice them to their gods. Fortunately, through the neglect of the guard placed over them, they managed to escape, and hurried back to the Spanish camp with their awful story. The Tlascalans were angry,

* An arrow tipped with red feathers was the sign of war.

and swore that they would sacrifice the Spaniards, and all who should assist them, to the gods; and were now gathering in vast numbers to stop their progress.

This news surprised Cortes. He had supposed that the warlike Tlascalans would have welcomed him as a strong ally to aid them in their opposition to Montezuma; and that, at least, their friendship with the Chempoallans and Totonacas would have made them his friends. He was at a loss to know the meaning of their conduct: perhaps his messengers had proved treacherous; possibly the Tlascalans might have supposed that he was a secret friend to Montezuma; or it might be that they had heard of what he had done in the temple at Chempoalla, and were determined upon revenge. These thoughts passed rapidly through his mind; but the truth is, he was wrong in all: he had mistaken the character of the Tlascalans. They were a warlike, independent people. They had once been governed by kings, but had shaken off the yoke, and formed themselves into a sort of republic. They had divided themselves into districts: each district had its separate ruler, who was elected by the people, and who represented his province in the general senate of Tlascala. It was not to be supposed that people who had thus struggled for independence and made a government of their own, would receive a band of armed strangers kindly, and had Cortes known as much of them, he would hardly have expected it.

But surprise could not help him. He knew that struggle was before him, and, without a sign of fear, he rallied his men for their march into Tlascala. Particular instructions were given to the different troops of his army, and then their beautiful standard was raised before them. Cortes, pointing to the banner, cried out, "Spaniards! follow boldly the standard of the Holy Cross, through which we shall conquer;" and the soldiers with one accord shouted, "On! on! in the name of God, in whom alone we place our trust."

After a march of two leagues, the Spaniards came to a stone wall, which in former days had been thrown up by the Tlascalans to stop the invaders from Mexico. Finding no enemy, they easily crossed the wall and pressed on. It was not long now before the advanced guard of the army saw some of the Tlascalan troops, and had a light skirmish. In a little time, as Cortes came forward with the main body, three thousand Tlascalans rushed from an ambush and poured in their arrows upon them. The Spaniards met this valiantly. After an obstinate struggle, the Indians were forced to give way and make their retreat. Yet Cortes marked that their retreat was made in an orderly and fearless manner, unlike the flight of most of the savages whom he had met; and he felt at once that he had to deal with no common Indians. He began therefore to be very particular in choosing the spots where his army should halt, and guarding the encampments through the night; and gave special command to the troops by no means to separate on their marches, but to proceed in solid and compact order.

The next day he was met by six thousand Tlascalans. These instantly attacked him, filling the air with their arrows, and making the plain echo with their yells, drums, and trumpets. But the cannons made sad havoc among them, and in a little time they gladly retreated to the top of a hill in the distance, from which they soon disappeared. Following on, Cortes reached at length the same height, when the whole Tlascalan army burst upon his sight. The plain far and wide was covered with the multitude. Forty thousand men were there, under the command of Xicotencatl, the general-in-chief of the Tlascalan republic. Undismayed by the numbers, he commanded his men to keep together at all hazards, and commenced at once descending the hill, amid flights of stones and arrows. They reached the plain: the cavalry and artillery were fairly brought into the action, and once more, after an hour's hard fight, the Tlascalans retreated before them. This was an unfortunate day for the Tlascalans; multitudes of their men were slain—how many, it is impossible to say, for, like all Indians, they carried off their dead to conceal their losses. Eight of their chiefs fell, while two were made prisoners. The Spaniards had fifteen men wounded, of whom only one died. One of their horses, however, was killed. The Indians carried the body away in triumph, and, cutting it in pieces, sent parts of it to all the cities of Tlascala.

Though victorious, Cortes was not satisfied with this hard struggle. The loss of one man was sorely felt by him; and he felt, moreover, that if other nations should by any chance join the Tlascalans, there was no hope of success to his enterprise. He desired peace, therefore, and accordingly sent his two prisoners to their countrymen with offers of peace. To this friendly message, Xicotencatl only sent back this bold answer:— "Bid them proceed to Tlascala, where the peace they shall meet from us shall be displayed by the sacrifice of their hearts and blood to the gods, and of their bodies to our feasts."

Cortes now very coolly informed his men that they were to make ready for another battle; and all that night they were busy in preparing their arms, ammunition, &c., and in making confession of their sins, and other acts of devotion. When morning dawned, they resumed their march, even the wounded men taking their places in the ranks. Ere long, they came again in sight of the

Tlascalan army. It covered the plain for two leagues: there were no less than fifty thousand men now gathered to oppose them; the army was made up of five divisions, each division being under the command of a chief, and the whole led on by the general Xicotencatl. His banner, bearing a large white bird like a spread ostrich, was proudly carried before him. As the Spaniards came near, the Indians commenced the battle with a tremendous discharge of arrows, darts, and stones, and then, amid shouts and yells as usual, rushed directly upon them. The artillery-men at once opened their cannons upon them, while the musketeers and crossbow-men kept up a continual fire, literally cutting down the multitude in heaps. Still the raging Tlascalans pushed onward without fear, and succeeded, for a moment, in breaking through the Spanish lines. It required all the courage and skill of Cortes to bring his men back to their position. The cavalry now rushed over the plain, sweeping down masses before them. Yet the brave Tlascalans pressed on with their numbers. Wherever a man fell dead, it seemed another arose with fiercer spirit to revenge his death. Thus the battle raged furiously on both sides. At length it was seen by the Tlascalans that one of their divisions kept out of the fight, nor could be pressed into it—the chief who headed it being provoked with Xicotencatl. This discouraged them:

they began to fall back, when one of their principal chiefs fell dead, and they were completely dismayed—the battle was ended. But for these circumstances, with all his skill and courage, Cortes had hardly prevailed against such numbers. It is very remarkable that in this fierce struggle the Spaniards had only one man killed. Seventy of their men, however, together with all their horses, were wounded. Some died of their wounds afterwards.

On the next morning, Cortes sent another message to the Tlascalans, demanding that he should be allowed to pass quietly through their territory, and threatening to desolate their whole country if they refused. But their fierce chiefs were not frightened: they did not yet feel that they were conquered, and determined to try his strength again. They now called together their priests, and demanded of them what could be the cause of their terrible defeat, and in what way they were to drive the invaders from their country. After performing many rites and sacrifices, the priests came forward and declared that the Spaniards were men like themselves, but were created by the heat of the sun in the regions of the East; that during the day they were not to be conquered, because they were guarded by the sun: at night they were not thus protected, and might then be easily overcome

The Tlascalans made ready again. Numbers soon gathered themselves, under the command of Xicotencatl, for an attack at night. As they drew near the Spanish camp, the sentinels marked them, the alarm was given, the cavalry rushed forth, and after another fight the astonished Tlascalans fled in dismay. They were now convinced that the Spaniards were *Teules*—the multitudes began to cry out that it was time to make peace; that the Spaniards were invincible. Another fierce message came from Cortes, and the senate was willing to have peace. Xicotencatl, in a rage, refused for a long time to come to any terms; he was not used to being conquered; but at last his proud spirit bent, and he consented to lay down his arms.

They were now at a loss to settle how they should approach the Spanish chief; they did not know what to think of him. He must be gentle and kind, for he sometimes released his prisoners of war, contrary to their way of sacrificing and eating them; then again they thought he must be cruel and bloodthirsty, for they remembered that fifty spies sent out by Xicotencatl had once approached his camp too closely, and, by his order, their hands were instantly cut off. Then, too, his fierce messages, and the tremendous slaughter that he had made among them, were calculated to frighten them. At length, forty of their chief men were started off, loaded with a variety of presents, some of which they hoped might please him, whatever he might be. As they came near, one of them advanced to Cortes, and said: "If you are *Teules*, as it is said, and desire human sacrifices, take the flesh of these slaves and eat: shed their blood and drink. If you are gods of a kind nature, here is a gift of incense and feathers; and if you are men, we bring you meat and bread for your nourishment." Soon after this, a large number of Tlascalans were seen approaching. Cortes supposed that they were coming for purposes of peace, yet instantly ordered his men to arms. Four of them now came forward with marks of profound respect, and offered him incense. They came, on the part of the Tlascalan senate, to make peace with him and his people. The Tlascalans (they declared) had opposed them only because they thought they were the friends of the cruel tyrant Montezuma, and were now sorry for it: they begged that they might be taken under the protection of Cortes. The Spanish chief quickly accepted their terms, and offered his protection and friendship to the whole republic. On the 23d of September (thirty-four days after reaching their territory), he triumphantly entered the city of Tlascala, the capital of their empire.

It was fortunate for Cortes that the war was thus ended, for some of his men were beginning to be dissatisfied; they had borne very cruel hardships. Every night half of them were on guard, while the other half only slept on their armor, ready to start up at any cry of danger. Fifty-five had perished since they entered the country, many were sick with diseases of the climate, and many were suffering from their wounds. Cortes was himself unwell, though he did not confess it. The number and fierceness of the Tlascalans, while it surprised all, had alarmed some, and these lived in the continual fear that they would be taken and sacrificed to the gods. It is not surprising, therefore, that murmurings commenced, and that many begged that they might return to Cuba. But when the Tlascalans surrendered, all were animated with new courage. Then the earnest friendship and submission of the Tlascalans (for Cortes was received very warmly in their capital) roused their drooping spirits the more. It is said that these Indians even reverenced the Spaniards now, saying that they were born in heaven. Certain it is that the horses and riders were looked upon as supernatural monsters: they believed that these monsters devoured men in battle, and that the neighing of the horses was their call for prey. Even when all was explained to them, they still held this belief. Their kindness and fears together drove away all discontent from the murmurers. No man sighed longer for the home left behind: all were greedy for the glory before them.

The submission of the Tlascalans prompted Cortes to speak to them about giving up their religion, with all its bloody rites; for, strange as it may seem when we look at some of his acts, Cortes never lost sight of the thought that the spread of the gospel was a part of the business of his enterprise. The Tlascalans refused, saying that while "the God of the Spaniards might be very great, they trusted in the gods of their forefathers." Upon this he was angry, and instantly prepared to carry out such a plan as before in the temple at Chempoalla. But Father Olmedo entreated that this might not be done. He declared that this was not the way to spread the gospel, and that he had looked on with horror at the scene in Chempoalla. Alvarado, Velasquez de Leon, and Lugo joined in the entreaty, and Cortes was at last persuaded not to attempt it His anger, however, served one good purpose. In the temples there were some poor wretches kept in cages, fattening for sacrifices, and Cortes caused all these to be set free.

Having allowed his men sufficient time to rest at Tlascala, Cortes determined to resume his march for Mexico. Some Mexicans now came forward and urged him to march through Cholula, a large town, where he would be kindly received. But the Tlascalans were opposed to this; they declared that the Cholulans were a treacherous people, devoted entirely to the interests of Montezuma, and that he would necessarily find himself there in the midst of enemies. Still Cortes resolved to pass through Cholula. He was anxious to please the Mexicans, and at the same time to teach the Tlascalans that he feared no enemy, whether concealed or open. With six thousand Tlascalans, therefore, in addition to his former numbers, he started for Cholula.

This town of Cholula was greatly celebrated for the temple of Quetzalcoatl that stood there. It was looked upon as the most sacred temple of the empire. Multitudes of pilgrims continually went there, and the sacrifices were almost daily. It is said that the Indians believed that this temple was built over secret springs of water, and that by pulling it down, these springs would burst forth into great rivers, and flood the whole surrounding country.* Some have supposed that this belief prompted the Mexicans to advise Cortes to go there : the secret springs of Quetzalcoatl were to be let loose, and prove the sure destruction of himself and his army.

As Cortes came near this town, the chiefs and priests marched out to meet him, bearing censers in their hands, and accompanied by a band of music. They received the Spaniards with pro-

* Torquemada ; Clavigero.

found respect; but when they saw the Tlascalans, they told Cortes plainly that all might enter their city except these, their old and bitter enemies. Cortes did not object to this; and at once ordering the Tlascalans to remain encamped outside, with great ceremony he entered Cholula. It was not a great while now before he began to be dissatisfied, and to suspect that the Tlascalans were right as to the character of these people; supplies of provisions began to be scantily furnished, and at last the Spaniards were left with nothing but wood and water. Ere long, some of the Chempoallans came to him and said that they had found secret pitfalls near the Spanish camp. These were large holes dug in the ground, having sharp stakes at the bottom, and covered over loosely with earth. Then some of the Tlascalans entered the city in disguise, and informed him that they had seen large numbers of women and children, loaded with valuable things, leaving the city by night; moreover, that six children had just been sacrificed in the temple, and this was a sure sign that the Cholulans intended something. Besides this, they had observed that many stones and darts had been collected on the tops of the temples. All this roused his suspicions very strongly. At length, Doña Marina came to him with certain information. She had learned the whole plan of the conspiracy. It seems that a Cholulan lady of high rank had become attached to her, and, desirous of saving her life, told her of the plot, that she might escape. Twenty thousand Mexicans were at a short distance from the city, ready at a certain signal to join the Cholulans in the general massacre of the Spaniards. Cortes instantly ordered some of the chief priests to be seized; and when they discovered that the Spaniards, or *Teules*, as they called them, knew everything, they confessed the whole. The enmity and treachery of the Cholulans were now certain.

In his indignation and rage, at the first moment, Cortes was at a loss what to do; at the next, he resolved upon signal vengeance. No time was to be lost. His principal officers were at once called together and told of the danger which threatened them, and his determination to be revenged. Some were for retreating to Tlascala, but most of them were ready heart and hand to join Cortes in his plan. He immediately ordered the Tlascalans to storm the city at the dawn of the next day, and to spare nothing but the women and children; and then informed the Cholulans that he intended to resume his march on the following morning.

These last were greatly delighted on hearing this, and they made haste to carry out their plot. At the break of day, the chiefs, with forty Cholulans, came into the open square in front of the Spanish encampment, and presently an immense number of troops rushed in and joined them. Cortes now mounted his horse and addressed them, telling them of the blackness and extent of their treachery. He knew all about it: the Spaniards (he said) had entered their city under a promise of friendship, and since their entrance had not done one unkind act towards the Cholulans; that they had behaved peaceably, and in every way proved that they meant no harm; that at their request he had even ordered a part of his army (the Tlascalans) to keep outside of the city; and he now understood very well what they meant by that request—it was only made to separate the Spaniards from their friends, that they might the more easily destroy them. "If (cried Cortes) you had a natural hatred to men from whom you had received no wrong, why not oppose us manfully and bravely in the field, like the Tlascalans, instead of resorting to means so cowardly and so treacherous to show your hatred and effect our destruction? The victory which your gods have promised you, is beyond their power; the bloody sacrifices which you expected to offer up to them, cannot be accomplished; and the end of this dark plot will only be to turn the intended ruin against the guilty heads of its contrivers."

The chiefs were completely confounded; they did not deny what he said, but at once commenced making excuses, saying that all was done by the order of Montezuma. But Cortes would have no excuse. He instantly ordered a musket to be fired; this was the signal to his men. The Spaniards sprang upon them, and the slaughter commenced; the whole square was soon a scene of horror. Multitudes were slain upon the spot, while some who fled only fell into the hands of the enraged Tlascalans, who were now pouring into the city. Some rushed to the temple of Quetzalcoatl and razed it to the ground, hoping that the waters would burst out and drown the Spaniards. But the rivers would not flow. They were in despair. Other temples were filled with crowds, entreating the gods to save them. The Spaniards now sallied from their quarters, and swept the streets with their artillery, literally piling them with the dead. Then they rushed to the temples, and demanded the poor wretches there to surrender. A proud and scornful answer was sent back to the summons: the temples were soon wrapped in flames; the Spaniards pressed on, and fire and sword soon completed the massacre. It is said that only one man surrendered; the rest choosing even to perish in the flames, or to throw themselves from the tops of the temples. Cholula was desolate: the streets rolled with the blood of six thousand men; dead bodies and half-burnt corpses lay scattered throughout them.

This horrid slaughter being ended, the Spaniards

and Tlascalans now commenced plundering the houses and stripping the temples of all that was left. The savage ferocity of these last was almost beyond bounds. At length the heart of Cortes was moved with pity; he looked upon the scene of havoc with horror. He now ordered Xicotencatl, who was there with twenty thousand men, to leave the place, as he should need him no longer; and then issued his proclamation, promising pardon to all who had escaped the massacre, and inviting them to return to their homes. Some were now seen creeping from the masses of the dead, where they had lain wounded, and women and children came in from the mountains where they had fled. The Tlascalans were made to deliver up all their prisoners, and peace was established between them and the Cholulans. Cortes then appointed a brother of the late Cacique (who had been killed in the massacre) to rule over the city, and in sorrow declared to the Cholulans who were left, that the treacherous conduct of their people had alone forced him to this terrible work of slaughter.

Well might Cortes be sorry for what was done. Six thousand of his fellow-beings lay butchered before him.* All that can be said for him is, that he may have thought his conduct necessary for his own safety, and perhaps the Tlascalans carried

* It is idle for Antonio de Solis to attempt to justify the action of Cortes; it is not to be justified.

the slaughter further than he intended. Yet this, which is all, is but a poor excuse for him. Perhaps it was his sorrow which prompted him earnestly to beg the Cholulans to leave off their bloody sacrifices and receive the Christian religion, and when they refused, to violate their temples no further than by setting free the poor wretches fastened in the cages for sacrifices.

CHAPTER V.

AFTER remaining a fortnight at the unfortunate town of Cholula, Cortes prepared to march on; but, before starting, called his officers together, and determined upon sending a messenger to Montezuma, to tell him that he was coming. The messenger was likewise directed to inform him that the Cholulans charged him with the guilt of their conspiracy, but that the Spanish general could not believe them, for he could not think that he would thus attempt to murder men who had done him no harm; that he had heard that Montezuma was a powerful king, and thought if he had any unkind feeling towards him, he would meet him boldly in the open field, and not resort to the cowardly meanness of stratagem; moreover, that the Spaniards were ready for any difficulty, whether their enemies were secret or open.

The messenger found Montezuma very unhappy. The news of the massacre at Cholula completely overcame him. He could not think without horror of allowing the Spaniards to enter his capital; and yet (poor undecided man!) in his fright and sorrow, he returned an answer, inviting Cortes to visit his city, and solemnly declaring that he had no part in the guilt of the Cholulans. The messenger had scarcely left, before he began to mourn bitterly over what he had done.

In the mean time, Cortes had left Cholula, and was rapidly advancing towards Mexico. He met with no opposition by the way. Wherever he passed, the people cheered him on; everywhere he heard from them bitter complaints of the tyranny of Montezuma, mingled with prayers that he would deliver them. The Spaniards felt great joy: they saw that the empire was divided; that the people, even in the very neighborhood of the capital, were dissatisfied and ready to rise. Pressing on with renewed spirit, they at length reached the top of Ithualco, when the beautiful valley of Mexico burst upon their sight. Now they were greatly delighted. As far as the eye could see, rich meadows, cultivated fields, and beautiful forests covered the plain. In the midst, like a sheet of silver, lay the lake Tezcuco, skirted around with pretty villages; while from its centre rose glittering in the sun the lofty temples and turrets of the city of Mexico. They looked upon the country which they had long panted to see, and felt that it was as beautiful as they had expected.

While the Spaniards had thus marched as far as Ithualco, Montezuma was in the heaviest sorrow—still undecided—not knowing what to do. The news of Cholula had so much overwhelmed him, that he had gone to the palace of Tlillancalmecatl, the place to which he always went when he would mourn and pray. Here he remained eight days, fasting, grieving, and going through with many religious services, to please the gods. From this place he sent another messenger to Cortes, entreating him not to enter the city of Mexico, and making him rich promises if he would comply with his request. He would pay a yearly tribute to the King of Spain, and he would give four loads of gold to Cortes, and one to each of his men. The messenger found Cortes at Ithualco, and delivered his message; but the Spanish chief only sent back the old answer—that he must see Montezuma, and deliver the message of his master Don Carlos.

Before his messenger had time to return, Montezuma (with his fears greatly increased by the dreams and traditions of which his priests had told him) called in his brother Cuitlahuatzin, and his nephew Cacamatzin, the lord of Tezcuco, to advise with them as to what he should do. His brother urged that the Spaniards should not be allowed to enter the city, while the nephew advised that they should. The advice of the latter was taken; and the Emperor ordered him to go out and meet the Spanish chief, and in his name to speak to him very kindly. At the same time he told him, if it were possible, to dissuade Cortes from entering the city.

Four noblemen were instantly started for Cortes, to inform him that Cacamatzin, the lord of Tezcuco, and nephew of the great Montezuma, was coming, and to beg that he would wait to receive him. In a little time, Cacamatzin appeared upon a splendid litter, borne by eight of his principal men, and surrounded by a crowd of Mexicans and Tezcucans. The Spaniards were wonderfully struck with the richness of this litter. It was adorned with jewels and pillars of gold, and from every golden pillar there were branches of rich green feathers. The noblemen helped Cacamatzin to alight, and then swept the ground before him as he moved towards Cortes. The Spanish chief received him with great respect; but when he spoke of Montezuma's wish, he received from Cortes the same stubborn answer that had always been given—that he must enter Mexico, and see the monarch himself.

Without waiting longer, Cortes pressed on towards the capital, along the causeway of Iztapalapan. He pretended on the way that he had friend ly feelings towards Montezuma, and expected to be kindly received by him; but at the same time was very cautious, as he moved along, to avoid any stratagem. At length he came to a place called Xoloc, about half a league from the city, where the main road to Mexico is met by that to Cojohuacan. At this place there was a fortress, crowned with two towers. Here he found great numbers of the people assembled to look upon him and his companions, the strange beings of whom they had heard so much. A long train of Mexican nobles, clothed in their richest dresses, now came forward, and passing before Cortes, made a low bow, at the same time touching the ground and kissing their hands. Passing this place, he had almost reached the city, when messengers came out to inform him that the great Montezuma was approaching. Presently, a long procession was seen. Three officers, each bearing a golden rod, walked before, giving notice to the people that the monarch was coming, while they instantly threw themselves upon the ground, in token of respect. Montezuma was next seen, sitting upon a splendid litter, borne by four noblemen on their shoulders. Then came two hundred noblemen, dressed in their rich cotton mantles, and wearing large plumes on their heads. These marched two by two, barefooted, with their eyes cast down to the ground, afraid to look up in the presence of the King. The Spaniards were amazed at the scene; Cacamatzin's appearance was forgotten in the splendor of this. The litter was covered with plates of gold, and surmounted by a splendid canopy of green feathers, beautifully ornamented with precious stones and golden fringes, while Montezuma himself was dressed most magnificently. He wore upon his head a crown of gold; upon his legs were gold buskins filled with precious stones; while, thrown loosely over his shoulders, hung a mantle bespangled with gold and gems. As he came near the Spanish chief, he was lifted from his litter, and borne upon the arms of the lords of Tezcuco and Iztapalapan, while the lords of Tacuba and Cojohuacan spread cotton mantles upon the ground, that the great King might not touch the earth with his feet. Cortes now dismounted his horse, and came forward with great respect, " addressing the King with deep reverence, after the fashion of Europe." Montezuma, following the fashion of his country, returned his compliment by touching the ground and then kissing it. Cortes then came near, and threw around his neck a thin collar of gold, strung with glass beads of different colors. This greatly pleased the King. Cortes would then have embraced him, but the nobles of Montezuma held him back.

This meeting raised the Spaniards greatly in the esteem of the Mexicans. Thousands had assembled to see it: the whole causeway was covered with the crowd, while the tops of houses and windows were filled with the multitude. Never before had they seen their great Emperor Montezuma do reverence to any man; for the first time in their lives, they saw him leave his palace, to greet with kindness a band of strangers. Naturally enough, they now thought the Spaniards were *Teules*, or deities indeed!

The feelings of the Spaniards were likewise strange. It was now the eighth day of November (seven months since their landing in the country), and they had at length reached the rich and beautiful city of Mexico. There it was, with its lofty domes and turrets, its splendid houses, and great masses of people. They felt already that they were rich. But with all this, they could not help thinking of other things. They were a band of four hundred and fifty men only, far away from home, in the heart of an unknown and populous country; they might enter that rich city only to be borne down by the multitudes; perhaps treachery might destroy them; the bridges of the causeways might be lifted, and all chance of escape be for ever cut off. Joy and anxiety filled their hearts.

They marched into the city more than a mile, before they came to the place which Montezuma had ordered to be made ready for their reception. This was the old palace of King Axajacatl, the father of Montezuma. Montezuma now took Cortes by the hand, and leading him to a large hall covered with tapestry and embroidered with gold and gems, said to him, " Malitzin, you and your companions are now in your own house: refresh and rest yourselves until my return." He, with all the Mexicans, then left him.

Cortes found his quarters very comfortable there was ample room for all his men, as well as his Indian allies. Montezuma had no sooner left, than he began to examine them with great care, to see that all was safe. He next ordered the artillery to fire their guns, by way of frightening the Mexicans, and then commenced putting his quarters in a state of defence. Guns were fixed in front of the gate, sentinels were posted round, and his men were commanded to act with the same prudence as though they were facing the camp of an enemy.

In a little time, Montezuma returned in the same splendid style as when he met Cortes on the causeway. He had brought with him rich presents for the Spanish general, and remained some time with him. It is said that he now told Cortes freely of his fears as regards the Spaniards; stating that it was not a great while since his ancestors came from the North, to rule the country only until Quetzalcoatl, the great god and lawful king, should return, and that these Spaniards (he believed) were his subjects. Cortes very artfully encouraged this belief in him, because he knew it would help his designs. At all events, he received the presents very kindly from Montezuma, and then talked to him of the greatness of his master Don Carlos. He was the greatest monarch in the world, and had sent him to make a treaty of friendship with the great Emperor of Mexico. He wished to alter certain laws and customs in his kingdom, and to offer him a religion far better than the bloody religion of Mexico. After the talk, they parted seemingly good friends on both sides.

The next day, Cortes, together with Alvarado, Sandoval, Velasquez de Leon, and Ordaz, paid a visit to Montezuma. They were received kindly, and the three following days were appointed by the Emperor for them to look at his capital. Their first visit in the morning was to the great square or market-place, Tlateloco. On one side, numbers of slaves were exposed for sale; on another, were vegetables, fruits, &c.; here were meats and poultry, and there were merchants selling all manner of furniture. The whole place was crowded with buyers and sellers, while perfect order was kept throughout. Three judges sat at one end of the square, while a number of officers moved through the crowd, to prevent riot or confusion. There were other small market-places scattered throughout the city, containing fountains, fish-ponds, and beautiful gardens; but this was the principal place for buying and selling in Mexico. From this place they went to the great temple of Mexico, passing through several large courts enclosed by heavy double walls, and paved with white cut stones. It seems that Montezuma, when he gave them permission to visit the city, had been afraid that the Spaniards might offer some violence to his gods in the temple, and consequently had gone there with many of his nobles. Cortes now met him. There were one hundred and fourteen steps to the temple—and Montezuma at once ordered six priests to lift Cortes up; but the Spaniard preferred walking up himself. When he reached the top of the platform, there were several large stones or altars for sacrificing, and at a little distance stood a horrid figure of a dragon, besmeared with blood. Montezuma came forward, and asked Cortes to look down upon his city now. From this high spot he could see everything: the whole city and surrounding country lay spread out before him. It was impossible to count the number of boats passing all the time between Mexico and the towns on the shore of the lake: and the crowds below in the streets of the city surprised Cortes more than ever. He now desired that he might see the principal gods of the temple, and after talking with his priests, Montezuma consented. The

Spaniards were now carried into a large hall, the walls of which were smeared with blood, and the roof curiously carved and ornamented. Here they saw two altars, richly dressed, and behind them the figures of two monstrous men. The face of one of these images expressed terrible passion and rage; his body was ornamented with precious stones, while an immense golden serpent was coiled around him. On his neck there was a collar, covered with heads and hearts wrought in gold. In his right hand he held a bow, in his left a bundle of arrows. Before him was a large fire, in which Cortes saw at the moment three human hearts burning. This was *Huitzilopochtli*, the god of war. By the side of the god, there was standing a little image, bearing a beautifully ornamented lance and shield : this was the page of the god. The other large figure had a face like a bear, with great shining eyes. In the fire before him there were five hearts. This was *Tezcatlipoca*, the god of providence, and brother of *Huitzilopochtli*. Next, on the top of the temple, he was shown the great religious drum. This was an immense drum, covered with the skin of a serpent. When this drum was struck, the doleful sound, it is said, could be heard for two leagues. Then they showed him the large knives for sacrifices, reeking with fresh blood, together with the horns and trumpets of the temple. Cortes now turned away in disgust, and demanded of Montezuma why he worshipped such monstrous idols, and allowed his people to be butchered before them. The King was very angry: he declared that Cortes should never have entered the temple, had he supposed that he would thus insult the gods. In a rage, he cried out—" Go, go hence, while I remain to appease the wrath of the gods, whom you have justly provoked by your blasphemous words!"

Cortes, with his companions, now passed out to a tower that was near by. At the entrance, which was always open, there were many idols, resembling serpents and other loathsome beasts. Upon entering, the Spaniards found in one part of the building piles of wood near a large reservoir of water, together with pots of water ready to boil the flesh of victims who were sacrificed, as food for the priests. In another part, were the tombs of the Mexican nobles; in another, were seen immense piles of human bones, curiously but regularly laid up. As in the temple, so in this tower priests were moving about in their long black mantles, with their ears cut and torn, and their long hair clotted with blood.

When Cortes again returned to his quarters, the Tlascalans came around him, talking earnestly of what they had often talked before—the treachery of Montezuma. They declared that he and his people were all crafty and treacherous: they knew them well; that the kind reception given to the Spaniards was only intended to deceive them; and that they believed they had been allowed to enter the city only that the bridges of the causeways might be lifted, all chance of escape cut off, and the whole of them be thus massacred. Moreover, that the Emperor was a fickle and uncertain man. Even if he was their friend now, he was likely, in some moment of passion, without any cause, to become their bitterest enemy. This increased the alarm which Cortes already felt about the same thing, for it was no news to him that Montezuma was treacherous. His own soldiers were ignorant of the fact, but Cortes perfectly understood it. Whatever Montezuma might say as to his innocence in the affair at Cholula, Cortes knew that he had made an effort to destroy his colony at Villa Rica. This he heard at Cholula, but carefully kept it from his men, fearful of discouraging them.*

It seems that after Cortes left that settlement, Montezuma sent to Quauhpopoca (the lord of Nauhtlan, a city on the coast) his secret orders to subdue the Totonacas, and punish them for their friendship to the Spaniards. The chief immediately attacked all their settlements. The poor Totonacas applied to the Spaniards at Villa Rica to help them. Juan de Escalante, who had charge

* This may help to explain the horrid massacre of Cholula.

at the post, instantly sent his orders to Quauhpopoca to cease troubling these Indians. Upon this, Quauhpopoca sent back for answer, that " if the Spaniards were disposed to take up the cause of the Totonacas, he was ready to meet them in the plains of Nauhtlan." Juan de Escalante now went out to meet him with fifty Spaniards, two thousand Totonacas, two cannons, and two horses. At the first attack of the Mexicans, the Totonacas fled. In spite of numbers, Escalante and his little band continued the fight: with their cannons, forced the Mexicans from the field, pursuing them and cutting many to pieces as far as the city of Nauhtlan. The victory was theirs, but they paid for it dearly: seven Spaniards and one horse were killed, and the brave Escalante, who was severely wounded, died three days afterward. One Spanish prisoner was taken, badly wounded. Fortunately, he died of his wounds, and thereby escaped being sacrificed. Quauhpopoca caused his head to be cut off, and after carrying it in triumph through many cities, to show the people that the Spaniards might be killed as well as others, at last sent it as a present to Montezuma.

Cortes had felt a deep sorrow for the death of Escalante; and the recollection of the cause of it, together with the suspicions of the Tlascalans, induced him now to seek some of his Indians whom he supposed were not prejudiced, and to inquire of them if they had seen anything like treachery on the part of the Mexicans. These thought that the common people showed no signs of it, but they were doubtful about others. Some of the nobles had been overheard saying that it would be an easy thing to break down the bridges on the causeways. It was likewise reported that Montezuma had seen the head of a Spaniard that had been sent to him by one of his generals, and then ordered it to be secretly taken away, that it might not be known to Cortes. This was, no doubt, the head of the poor Spaniard sent by Quauhpopoca.

Cortes was now greatly alarmed; he felt assured that treachery was at work. With a heart full of anxiety, he went to his quarters, where he spent the whole night walking to and fro over the floor. A thousand plans floated through his mind: none pleased him; yet it was necessary to act promptly and decidedly. At last a thought crossed him, the very boldness of which made even Cortes shudder. His plan was formed. He would seize Montezuma himself, and make him a prisoner. This would secure his safety; the Mexicans would hardly attempt any act of violence when the life of their King was in his hands. He and his brave companions might perish in the attempt, but it were better to die in it than to be cut to pieces retreating, or be massacred in the streets of Mexico. The next morning, by his command, all his officers were assembled. Cortes now told them of the danger which threatened them. He declared that Montezuma was treacherous; the affair at Villa Rica, and consequent death of Escalante, plainly showed it; that even now his treachery was at work; the Tlascalans had suspected it, but it was now proved; his nobles had been overheard, secretly talking of breaking down the bridges. For his part, he was resolved upon what he would do. The danger was great, the remedy hazardous; but he would die or accomplish it. He would seize Montezuma, and bring him a prisoner to his quarters. The officers were startled by this bold declaration. Some cried out that it was impossible: if undertaken, it would prove the sure destruction of all the Spaniards; others thought it best to retreat back to Villa Rica as fast as they could; but Velasquez de Leon and Sandoval agreed with their leader, saying that it could and must be done. The matter was talked over a long time, until at last they all agreed that the plan of Cortes should be executed at all hazards.

Cortes now proceeded with great prudence. It would not do to march with his soldiers in a body to the palace of the King: this would at once rouse the Mexicans. He chose, therefore, Alvarado, Sandoval, Velasquez de Leon, Lugo, and Davila, five of his best tried officers, together with five of his bravest soldiers, to accompany him.

Twenty-five picked men were to follow on at intervals, strolling along as though they were brought to the palace by accident. Christoval de Olid and Diego de Ordaz were placed in command of all the soldiers left behind, with orders to be ready to rush out at the first alarm.

He now marched to the palace. Without suspicion, he was admitted, and received kindly by the King. In a little time, Cortes began, in a very severe way, to upbraid him about the conduct of Quauhpopoca. It was by his advice (he said) that his people at Villa Rica had been disturbed. He believed now that he was also guilty of contriving the plot of Cholula, and was sorry to find so great a monarch acting so meanly. He had not spoken of this before, from motives of prudence, but now that he had discovered another plot preparing in Mexico, he came to assure him that he should protect his men at all hazards. When Doña Marina and Aguilar interpreted the language of the general, Montezuma changed color, and was for some time speechless. At length he spoke, solemnly declaring that he was innocent. He had given no orders to Quauhpopoca to trouble the Spaniards. Then taking from his wrist the signet of *Huitzilopochtli*, he gave it to some of his officers, with a positive command to seize Quauhpopoca and bring him to Mexico. Cortes now expressed himself well pleased ; in his own mind (he said) he was satisfied of his innocence. But the Spaniards were dissatisfied and alarmed, and ready to rise. One thing alone he believed could pacify them, and make them feel perfectly safe: that was, for Montezuma to leave his palace, and take up his abode in the Spanish quarters. Montezuma was now enraged; he could scarcely speak. He cried out, that he would never thus humble himself; that the Kings of Mexico were not used to surrendering themselves prisoners without a struggle; and if he were base enough to do so, his people would rise in a mass. Cortes, in reply, expressed his surprise that the King should think himself a prisoner, for removing to the Spanish quarters; that it was only returning to the palace of his old father Axajacatl, and that the Mexicans could neither be alarmed nor surprised at it. But no persuasion could move him; he was firmly resolved not to go. Velasquez de Leon, seeing his resolution, now cried out very angrily, "Why should we waste more time in words? He must yield himself our prisoner, or we will forthwith stab him to the heart! Let us secure our lives, or perish at once." His fierce and threatening manner startled Montezuma. He turned to Doña Marina, and asked what that fierce Spaniard meant. She at once answered, "Prince, I am your subject, and am anxious for your safety; but, as the friend of these strangers, I know their characters. Yield to their request, and they will treat you with every kindness; refuse it, and they will not hesitate to take your life." Montezuma was now completely subdued, and readily consented to go. "Let us, then, depart to your quarters," he said; "the gods have decreed it so, and I trust myself to your honor." Cortes now caused him to call some of his lords, and inform them that it was his choice and pleasure to make his home in the Spanish quarters. He was then placed upon his splendid litter, and carried from his palace. The Mexicans, hearing what was done, were greatly roused: they thought the Spaniards were stealing away their King, and made awful threats against them. But when they saw the litter passing through the streets, surrounded by the officers of the Emperor, and Montezuma waved his hand to them in token of command, they were at once satisfied and quiet.

9*

CHAPTER VI.

IN a little time, Montezuma became quite satisfied in the Spanish quarters. He was treated as the King of Mexico, and his government went on as usual. His chiefs were allowed to visit him, and his nobles served up for him his splendid feasts as before in his own palace. It is said, that after feasting, he would frequently send what was left as a present to the Spanish soldiers. They shared his kindness in another way. He became very fond of Cortes and Alvarado, and amused himself by playing with them a game called bodoque, and all his winnings at the game were given to the soldiers. Naturally enough, this kindness, together with the commands of Cortes, induced the men to treat him with great respect. Cortes was very strict on this point; he had one of his men, on one occasion, severely whipped, for using rude words toward the monarch. Montezuma was also allowed to visit the temple, and go out upon the chase sometimes; but on these occasions he was always attended by a body of Spaniards, to prevent his being rescued. Though a prisoner, he was still the King, and felt happy.

This happiness did not last long, however. At the end of a fortnight, Quauhpopoca and some of his companions in the attack on Escalante were brought prisoners to Mexico. Though a prisoner, Quauhpopoca was borne upon a splendid litter like a conquering hero. He at once sought Montezuma, and presented himself before him as one who had faithfully obeyed his orders. To his surprise and confusion, the King treated him coldly, and ordered him to be delivered immediately to Cortes. He was now put to the torture, and confessed that all he had done was by command of his King. A court, made up of Spaniards, then tried him, and condemned him to be burnt alive. Cortes went now to Montezuma, and told him of the confession of Quauhpopoca, and the punishment he was to suffer; adding, very sternly, that he too would be put to death but for his late acts of kindness: his life would be spared, but that he was not to escape all punishment for his treachery. With that, he ordered a Spaniard, who had brought a pair of iron fetters along, to fasten them upon the legs of Montezuma. It was instantly done, and Cortes left him, to punish Quauhpopoca. The poor King of Mexico was confounded and speechless. His nobles who attended him clung to his fetters, and wept bitterly.

Cortes now gathered a large quantity of bows, arrows, and darts, from the Mexican armory, and caused an immense fire to be made of them directly in front of Montezuma's palace. Quauhpopoca and three other chiefs (some say fifteen others) soon perished in the flames. Thousands of Mexicans looked calmly upon the scene; no resistance was made, for they thought it was all done by the command of the King. This horrible act being ended, Cortes again went to Montezuma, spoke kindly to him, and with his own hands took off his fetters. To carry his kindness further, he now told him that he was at liberty, and might return, if he pleased, to his own palace. This last was only a pretence of kindness, for Cortes knew very well that Montezuma dared not go. The people had just seen the death of the brave general Quauhpopoca, and Montezuma knew that he would probably suffer for the guilt of it.

Though the Mexicans made no resistance at the time, the insolent bearing of the Spaniards, before the very palace of their King, had roused the anger of many. The proud spirit of Cacamatzin, the lord of Tezcuco, was greatly excited. He at once gathered together a body of the nobles at

Tezcuco, and they resolved to declare war upon the Spaniards. They were quickly busy in making their preparations, and the rumor of their intentions soon spread. Cortes began to feel alarmed for his safety, and Montezuma began to be startled with the thought of losing his crown; for, with the rumors, came the story that Cacamatzin intended to seize the reins of government, thinking that his uncle had disgraced both himself and the empire. They both sent messengers to Cacamatzin, commanding him to leave off his warlike preparations; but Cacamatzin only sent back this proud answer: " That his country was disgraced; that the Spaniards could no longer deceive or frighten him; they must leave Mexico, and return to their own country, or take the storm that was gathering." Cortes now proposed to march out and attack him. Montezuma, however, advised him not to do this, stating that Tezcuco was a strongly-fortified city, the second in the empire, and he would only perish in the attempt. He sent, therefore, another message to his nephew, inviting him to come up to the capital and visit him, at which time all difficulties might be happily settled. Cacamatzin was now more indignant than ever: he declared to his followers that his uncle was more a friend to the strangers than to his own people. He sent for answer this time, that he would come to the capital, but not to waste words in idle talk : he would come to destroy the Spaniards. Finding his nephew thus resolute, Montezuma now determined to make him a prisoner. He took his signet from his arm, and giving it to some of his nobles, commanded them secretly to seize his rebel nephew, and bring him a prisoner to Mexico. His order was soon carried out. In a little time, the nobles returned, bringing Cacamatzin. Montezuma rebuked him, and then delivered him to Cortes. He was at once thrown into prison, and his brother Cuitcuitzcatzin sent out in splendid style to take charge of the province of Tezcuco.

Made bold by his success in this matter, Cortes now resolved that Montezuma should declare himself subject to the King of Spain. He went to him, and told him that it was his desire that he should acknowledge the authority of the King of Spain over him, and subject his kingdom to a yearly tribute in token of dependance. The poor captive monarch, in great sorrow, soon assented to this. He called all his lords and nobles together in a great hall in the Spanish quarters. With sobs and tears, he reminded them of the old tradition that the sons of Quetzalcoatl were to come and rule the Mexican empire ; that he held it, as they knew, only till that time ; the time was now come ; the Spaniards (he believed) were the sons of Quetzalcoatl, and he was ready to recognise the title of the King of Spain over his dominions. His chiefs and lords heard this declaration in silent grief; yet they gave their consent; for, like the King, they believed the tradition: they were afraid to resist. Montezuma informed Cortes that on the next day they would all swear allegiance to the Spanish King. Accordingly, on the day following, it was done in the presence of all the Spanish officers, and even their hearts (it is said) were moved when they witnessed the sorrow of Montezuma as he took that oath.

One step led on to another. Cortes next resolved to persuade him that it was right and proper that his empire should send a rich present of jewels, gold, and silver, to the King of Spain. It was soon done. To this also he assented: he brought forward his own treasures liberally, at the same time sending commands to all his lords throughout the kingdom to bring in their portions. Within twenty days, an amount equalling six hundred thousand dollars, besides jewels, was collected at Mexico. Cortes now proceeded to divide this treasure. One fifth part was for the King of Spain; one fifth part for himself; from the balance was to be taken what he, Velasquez, and others, had expended in fitting out the expedition; and then the remainder was to be equally divided among the men, according to their rank. The soldiers were dissatisfied with this division, especially the part given to the King of Spain, who had never aided them in any way in the enterprise; but Cortes managed to pacify them by giving secret presents to some, and offering promises and prospects to all.

The Spanish chief had rolled upon a tide of fortune thus far; but now it began to turn. Matters had come to such a pass, that some of the Mexican nobles, forgetting their traditions and their fears, began seriously to think of forcing the Spaniards from Mexico. Their King was a captive, Quauhpopoca murdered, Cacamatzin in prison, their gods insulted, and the whole country, in fact, under the control of strangers. This was more than could be borne. They began to hold secret meetings, and sometimes to meet Montezuma secretly. Matters were freely talked over: the priests, who hated the Spaniards, threw in their advice, and all this ended in a solemn resolution that the Spaniards should leave the city. They were afraid, however, to attack them openly, so long as Montezuma was in their possession. They were to be got off peaceably, if possible, and therefore another plan was adopted. Montezuma sent for Cortes, and told him that "he had already been in his capital six months, and there was no reason in his remaining any longer. He wished him, therefore, to depart as speedily as possible. His priests, his nobles, and his people were all dissatisfied, and determined that the Spaniards should no longer remain in the land. Moreover, that it was the will of the gods that the strangers who had insulted them should be expelled, or sacrificed." This was said very sternly by the King, and Cortes, who had heard that a conspiracy was at work, felt that it must be strong when Montezuma could speak to him so boldly. He knew, too, if the Mexicans did rise against him, it was death to his hopes. He very artfully, therefore, answered the King that his demand was very reasonable; that he had himself already thought of leaving Mexico. He could not, however, leave immediately; his ships had been destroyed, and it was necessary to build new ones. He hoped the Mexicans would allow him time to make his preparations. Montezuma was greatly pleased. The thought of his departure was real joy to him. He embraced Cortes, and promised him not only time to make his preparations, but that he would assist him in making them. He sent out his order that some of his men should at once go to the woods to cut timber for the Spaniards, and that some of his carpenters should set to work in helping them to build their ships. Cortes left Montezuma feeling very happy himself; he saw he had deceived the King: he had no thought of leaving the country, and was hoping, during the time allowed him, that he might gain strength in some way to meet any difficulty. At the end of a week, however, ships appeared on the coast. Montezuma, hearing of this, sent for him again, and told him there was no necessity for his remaining any longer to build his vessels; ships were off the coast, and he must start immediately.

Cortes felt more joy than sorrow. The news of the ships delighted him; he thought instantly of Portocarrero and Montejo, the messengers whom he had sent to Spain to get the authority of Don Carlos. Nine months had passed away since they left him; he had looked for them eagerly before, and supposed they had now arrived with fresh troops to help him in his conquest. In this he was sadly disappointed. The truth was, that his very messengers had betrayed him. Contrary to their positive orders, they had stopped at Cuba, on their way to Spain. Portocarrero being sick, Montejo had forced the pilot, Alaminos, to touch at Havana, under pretence of getting supplies from his estate. The ship had no sooner cast anchor, than he sent a sailor ashore with letters to Velasquez. The Governor was more enraged than ever; from that moment, he had used all his efforts to ruin Cortes. The eighteen ships on the coast were under the command of Pamphilo de Narvaez, and he had been sent out by him, at the head of eight hundred soldiers, with positive orders to seize Cortes and his principal officers, and send them prisoners to Cuba. It was not long before Cortes understood the whole.

Narvaez had made a landing on the coast of Chempoalla, and was soon joined by three Spanish deserters. These told him that Cortes was in a forlorn and wretched condition, and might easily be taken. Narvaez was made bold by such news. He immediately sent off Guevara, a priest, with a company, to Sandoval (who was commanding at Villa Rica since the death of Escalante), to demand that he should surrender that place. Sandoval refused to do so, and when the priest proved insolent, told him that his sacred order alone protected him. Upon this, Guevara was very angry: the quarrel became high, and Sandoval seized him and his companions, and sent them prisoners to Mexico. Upon their arrival there, Cortes very prudently received them kindly; he took off their fetters, expressed himself sorry for the conduct of Sandoval, made them many rich presents, and in this way completely won them over as friends. They now talked to him freely of Narvaez and the strength of his forces: said that he had declared to the Indians that Cortes was a traitor and tyrant, keeping their King a prisoner, and that he was sent out by the King of Spain to set them free. They stated, too, that Montezuma was sending secret messages to him, and that several of the Mexican provinces had openly declared in his favor.

Cortes was now in a very dangerous and trying position. It was idle for him to march out and meet Narvaez with all his fresh and numerous troops; to release Montezuma, and attempt to retreat from Mexico, would prove sure destruction; to remain where he was, in an enemy's city, and wait for Narvaez to attack him, would prove equally unsafe. His courage, however, did not forsake him. He was resolved upon one thing—that he would never leave as a prisoner the country that he had entered as a conqueror, and never allow another to reap the glory which he thought he had earned. Narvaez was, he supposed, his most dangerous enemy, and he turned his thoughts towards him. He made up his mind that before long he must come to a battle with him, but, in the mean time, he would try to win him as a friend: if he failed in that, he would try to break up his strength by bringing over some of his officers. He selected, as the messenger whom he would send to him, Father Olmedo, whose prudence he had tried before this. He was to propose terms of friendship; if he failed in carrying this point, he was to use his arts in making friends in his army. Accordingly, Olmedo was sent off with letters to Narvaez and some of his officers—among the rest, Andres de Duero, the old friend of Cortes, who was fortunately one of them—together with many rich presents for them from Cortes.

Narvaez received him with great scorn. He declared that he would soon cut off the head of the traitor Cortes, and put all his followers to death. It was in vain that Father Olmedo reasoned with him, telling him that the Spaniards were brothers; that the glory of their common country required that they should turn their forces against the Mexicans, and that Cortes was ready to do so. Narvaez would hear no terms of peace whatever. Finding that he failed in this point, Olmedo remembered the other. He mingled with the men, talked with them freely, delivered the rich presents of Cortes, and soon won over some of the officers. Fortunately, just at this time, Guevara and his companions returned. They talked loudly of the generosity of Cortes, and the glory that was before the Spaniards, if they would only join forces; declaring that no better leader could be found than Cortes, and that it was a shame to take the command from him after all his perils. Narvaez, only the more enraged at all this, ordered Guevara never again to speak to him of terms of friendship between him and Cortes, and immediately issued his proclamation, declaring Cortes and all his followers rebels to Don Carlos, and traitors to their country.

Upon Olmedo's return, Cortes felt at once that he was to have a struggle with Narvaez, and that the sooner it was met the better. Leaving one hundred and fifty of his men, therefore, at Mexico, under the command of Alvarado, with particular instructions to guard Montezuma closely, he started with the remainder of his forces to meet him What he most feared was the cavalry of Narvaez. To enable his soldiers to meet these, he sent Tobilla to Chinantla to get from the Cacique three hundred of the long spears used by his warriors in battle. He pushed on very rapidly towards Chempoalla, having no baggage or artillery to delay him. At Tapanacuetla (a village thirty miles from that place), he was joined by Sandoval and his men from Vera Cruz. His whole force now amounted only to two hundred and fifty men; yet they were brave men, ready to face any danger. Determined, if possible, not to shed the blood of his countrymen, Cortes once more sent Father Olmedo to bring Narvaez to terms of peace. Again he was received with scorn, and again set himself to the work of intriguing with the men. Another messenger was now sent; this was Velasquez de Leon. It seems that Narvaez had counted surely upon his friendship, remembering that he was a kinsman to Velasquez, and had written him a letter, urging him to join him. This Velasquez de Leon had very proudly and indignantly refused to do. Cortes was greatly delighted with this proof of his friendship; and thinking it would help his cause, now sent De Leon also a messenger to Narvaez. He was received with great attention. Narvaez made him brilliant offers: he should be second in command, and earn great glory, if he would only abandon Cortes. Velasquez de Leon again refused, declaring that he would die, sooner than desert such a noble commander as Cortes; that he had already earned great glory for his country; and as he had begun the conquest, he was the best man to finish it. Narvaez and some of his officers were now very angry, and spoke abusively of Cortes and his followers. This was more than De Leon could brook; he was enraged at hearing his brave companions thus spoken of, and laid his hand upon his weapon. Fortunately, some of the more prudent Spaniards came forward at this moment, and urged him and Father Olmedo to leave the camp. They left, but many friends were left behind them. The soldiers of Narvaez had begun to look upon their leader as obstinate and stubborn. The messengers had scarcely gone, when, in a rage, he offered a reward of two thousand crowns for the heads of Cortes and Sandoval. Hearing, too, that Cortes had been bold enough to come within a league of Chempoalla, he at once set his army in motion to give him a battle.

Fortunately for Cortes, one of Narvaez' men deserted his camp, and informed him of what was done. Narvaez had drawn up his whole army in a large plain near Chempoalla, and determined there to wait for him. Cortes was not so imprudent as to meet him there with his little handful of men. He kept quiet, therefore, on the other side of the river Canoas, which runs near Chempoalla, determined to wait for some better opportunity. A heavy fall of rain now set in, and the soldiers of Narvaez, unaccustomed to hardships, began to murmur and complain. It was idle, they said, to remain in such a storm; Cortes and his few followers would not dare to approach them at such a time. Some of the officers joined with them, and persuaded Narvaez to take them back to their quarters in Chempoalla. Having carried them back he posted two sentinels at the ford of the river to watch the enemy, and sent a number of horsemen to keep a lookout upon the road leading to the town, and to move around his quarters. In the mean time, Cortes and his little army stood drenched in the rain without a murmur; every man seemed happy and contented. Naturally supposing that Narvaez and his men would be weary and unsuspicious of his approach after such a day, he determined to attack them at midnight, while they were all in their quarters. Accordingly, he called his little band around him, told them of his design, and made a stirring speech to them. He spoke of the sufferings and dangers they had borne the victories they had won, and the glorious prospects before them; and now he said they had been declared rebels and traitors by their unnatural countryman Narvaez. As he went on, he was interrupted by the shouts of the soldiers; and when he finished, they all declared that they would follow such a leader for ever. Some went so far (it is said) as to swear they would kill Cortes if he tried again to make peace with Narvaez. He thanked them for their love, and warmly praised their courage. His little army was now divided into three parties. The command of the first was given to Sandoval. This had the most difficult duty to perform: it was to seize the artillery of the enemy, and Cortes placed in it, therefore, some of his picked men. The second division was intrusted to Christoval de Olid: he was to storm the town, and take possession of Narvaez. Cortes himself led the third party: this was to act as a body of reserve, and rush to the support of either party that required it. The rain had swollen the river so much, that it was dangerous to pass it; yet, with the waters rising to their breasts, they all crossed the ford. Every man being armed with his sword, dagger, and spear, they now moved on silently and in regular order. The guard in advance fortunately caught one of the sentinels, but the other fled to the city and gave the alarm. This caused Cortes to move on more rapidly. But Narvaez would not believe the sentinel; he thought it impossible that Cortes should be moving on such a night, and rebuked him as a coward who had been frightened. No horsemen were seen to interrupt him on the road (they were probably tired, and had taken shelter from the rain), and thus Cortes reached at midnight, unobserved, the principal temple of Chempoalla, where Narvaez held his quarters. A long row of artillery guarded the entrance to the temple, but no time was to be lost. Cortes gave the signal for attack. Sandoval and his brave followers rushed forward so fiercely, that the enemy only fired three guns, when they were forced to take to their other weapons. He now drove them back from their guns, and, amid a shower of arrows and balls, began to press his way up the steps of the temple. Numbers poured out and crowded the steps; still Sandoval kept the guns, and maintained his ground at great hazard, in spite of all opposition. Narvaez was not idle; he was up, and rallying his men. Christoval de Olid and Cortes now rushed to the assistance of Sandoval, bearing down everything before them. Sandoval reached the temple-door, and tried to burst it open, but failed. In the mean time, one of the soldiers had fired the tower: it was in a blaze; multitudes were rushing from it. Sanchez Farzan, one of the soldiers, now struck Narvaez with his spear. He instantly fell, was seized, dragged down the steps, and fastened with fetters. The news was soon spread that Narvaez was dead: shouts of victory rang through the air; his followers were confounded. His soldiers in the two smaller towers were in the greatest confusion. In their fright and consternation, they even took the fire-flies, in the darkness, to be soldiers' matches; all was despair. In spite of the entreaties of Diego Velasquez and Salvatierra, they laid down their arms and surrendered. The battle was ended; the prisoners were all put under the charge of Sandoval, who had them carried to a safe place, under a guard of picked soldiers.

The next morning found Cortes a conqueror, seated on a chair, surrounded by all his brave officers. The conquered officers passed before him, and kissed his hand. Right glad were they to make a friend of him now. He now sent Lugo to the fleet to bring off the pilots and sailors, and then to dismantle the ships, to prevent any one from returning to Cuba. Next he ordered all the prisoners to be set free, except Narvaez and Salvatierra, and then offered to send them all back to Cuba, or take them as his soldiers. The men had seen his bravery: they now saw his generosity; his followers, too, seemed to have plenty of gold and trinkets; and, almost to a man, they consented to join him. They felt that glory was before them, and that Cortes was the commander to lead them on. He was now fairly at the head of an army, together with one hundred horses, plenty of ammunition, and abundance of military stores.

CHAPTER VII.

SCARCELY was the victory won, when a courier arrived in hot haste from Alvarado. The Mexicans had risen in the capital; two brigantines, which Cortes had built to command the lake, were destroyed, —seven Spaniards had been killed,—and Alvarado was now closely besieged in his quarters. Cortes was greatly startled by these sad tidings. He knew that the force of Alvarado, though brave, was small, and instantly commenced preparations for his departure. In the midst of these, two other messengers arrived, heaping curses upon Alvarado, declaring that his rashness and folly alone had brought about this disaster.

It seems that Cortes had scarcely left Mexico, when the inhabitants of that city began to think of attacking his countrymen. They knew that he was the great leader of the Spaniards, and thought that during his absence they might rescue Montezuma, and revenge themselves thoroughly. Many secret meetings had been held by them for the purpose of completing their plans, and all was nearly ripe for action, when the Spaniards discovered the plot. They were all greatly enraged: none more so than their leader Alvarado. Still they behaved prudently; and, but for the hasty violence of Alvarado, all might for some time have been kept quiet. The principal festival of the Mexicans (that of *Huitzilopochtli*, the god of war) came on just at this time. At this festival, which was always celebrated with great magnificence, it was customary for the King, the nobles, the priests, and the people, to join in certain dances. The nobles, having requested Alvarado to allow Montezuma to join them, and been refused, prepared now to keep the festival without him. The Mexicans had all assembled in the large court of the great temple, the dancing and singing had commenced, when Alvarado (thinking this a fit occasion for striking terror in the hearts of the conspirators) ordered his soldiers out, and rushed furiously upon them. So sudden was the attack, that numbers of the Indians were at once massacred. In a little time, however, they rallied, and prepared for a desperate revenge. Nothing could now restrain them; not even the thought of what might befall Montezuma could allay their fury. They rushed upon the Spanish quarters, battering the walls, and destroying most of their ammunition. Alvarado and his little force made a gallant resistance, and were still making it, but were now fairly besieged, and had before them every prospect of perishing, either by war or famine.

Cortes hurried his preparations, and all was soon ready. He made an oration to the followers of Narvaez, to inspire them with courage, and then intrusting Narvaez and Salvatierra to the keeping of Rodrigo Ranzel, whom he appointed his lieutenant at Villa Rica, set out on his rapid march for Mexico. At Tlascala he was joined by two thousand warriors, and he now felt strong enough to curb the fury of the Mexicans. He passed on rapidly to Tezcuco; but scarcely had he entered the Mexican territories, when he saw at once many signs of Mexican feeling. No welcome met him as usual in any of the towns through which he passed: they all seemed deserted; nor was any provision made anywhere for the comfort of himself or his army. He was unmolested, however, in his march, and at length, on the 24th of June, 1520, again entered Mexico. Here, again, no one came forward to meet him: a gloomy silence seemed to reign through the city. Cortes felt assured now that difficulties were before him; yet, strange to tell, his first act was one of imprudence. When at length he reached Montezuma, and the King would have complimented him on his victory over Narvaez, he turned away from him with scorn. Perhaps he felt that he had force enough now to carry his point at all hazards, or possibly he thought that Montezuma was treacherous; that he was aiding the fury of his people. Alvarado was instantly summoned before him, to give an account of all that had happened. He declared that a priest and two nobles had informed him that the Mexicans had entered into a plot to destroy the Spaniards; moreover, that news had reached the capital that Cortes and his army had been vanquished by Narvaez; that this had emboldened them: they were ripe for action; to protect himself, he could make no delay, and therefore had fallen upon them at the time of the festival. It is said that Cortes was dissatisfied with this explanation. Still, this was no time for finding fault: Alvarado and his companions were in trouble, and their only hope of relief was through him. He was provoked at the boldness of the Mexicans, and especially so when he found they furnished no supplies for his army. He bore himself very haughtily toward the nobles wherever he met them, and at length sent a very stern message to Montezuma, commanding him immediately to supply his troops with provisions. This message only roused the Mexicans the more; and from that moment they commenced a war of indomitable hatred against all Spaniards.

Ere long, a Spanish soldier came rushing into the quarters, and fell down, sinking with the loss of blood. This poor fellow had been sent by Cortes, to bring to Mexico the daughter of Montezuma and other ladies left at Tacuba, under the care of the Cacique. The enraged Mexicans had attacked him on the causeway, and he had escaped only by the most desperate exertions. He declared that the whole country was in arms, and that multitudes from all quarters were moving toward Mexico. Cortes immediately sent out Diego de Ordaz, with four hundred men, to reconnoitre. These Spaniards had scarcely moved into the streets, when they were attacked with showers of arrows, while the air was filled with the loud curses and threats of the Mexicans. "Every man of them should be sacrificed to the gods: not one Spaniard should escape; and every Tlascalan should share the same fate." The streets were filled with the phrensied multitude, while, from the tops of the houses and temples, darts, stones, and arrows, were poured upon the Spaniards. Ordaz found that he could neither move forward nor readily retreat; he was completely hemmed in by the throng. His courage, however, did not forsake him; with a desperate energy, he fought his way back to the Spanish quarters, twenty-three of his men having been killed, and a large number wounded. This success only emboldened the Mexicans. The next day they came in vast numbers to attack the Spanish quarters. A wild madness seemed to possess them. The artillery was at once brought to bear upon them, and, though masses were swept down in the streets at every volley, the places of the dead were instantly supplied by others; there seemed no end to their numbers. Twice they came near forcing an entrance into the quarters. Disappointed in this, they at length set fire to them, and the Spaniards were enabled to stop the flames only by throwing down one of the walls to extinguish them.

Another difficulty now presented itself, in the disaffection of the soldiers of Narvaez. They were startled by the threats and fury of the Mexicans; they had followed Cortes, not expecting such disasters, and began now to murmur loudly. It was no time to listen to their complaints. To inspire them with confidence, Cortes resolved upon a bold effort. With a handful of men, he made in person a desperate sally upon the enemy; but, in spite of his bravery, was forced to retreat, leaving ten of his men dead in the streets, and about fifty wounded. His energies, however, increased with his difficulties. He resolved upon another attack. Perceiving that his men suffered most from the darts and arrows thrown from the roofs of the houses, he caused them to make four machines, called *mantas*. These machines were made of strong timbers, covered with a roof, and moved on wheels. Each one could carry about thirty soldiers. Thus prepared, he again sallied out at the head of most of the Spaniards and two thousand Tlascalans. The Indians hailed them as usual with shouts of fury and defiance, pouring in upon them clouds of arrows. Expecting this attack, they had prepared to annoy the Spaniards in every way. In some places, the streets were blocked up to prevent their passage; in others, the bridges that crossed the canals in the city were broken down; and while the Spaniards were stopped from time to time by these obstacles, they assailed them furiously from the streets, the canals, the roofs and windows of the houses. As for the *mantas*, they afforded but little protection, for the ingenuity of the Indians soon destroyed them. From the tops of the houses they hurled down immense stones and broke them to pieces. The priests were in the midst, inflaming the people; the nobles, by their example, urged them on, and they fought desperately. The battle was waged fiercely on both sides through the whole day. Worn out at last by the continued attacks carried on from the houses, Cortes ordered his men to fire the city. Several houses were soon burnt to the ground, and he now retreated to the Spanish quar ters as rapidly as possible. It was a sad day to both parties. Multitudes of the Mexicans were slaughtered, while forty Spaniards were slain, and a large number wounded. Cortes was himself badly wounded in the hand in this conflict.

Cortes now felt that his position was most dangerous. He could neither conquer nor make terms of peace, nor hope for a quiet retreat. To attempt a retreat from the capital was all that seemed left to him: to remain where he was, was courting almost certain death by war or famine; and yet he could not brook the thought of being anything but a conqueror, after all his toils and struggles. Fortunately, at this time he had a prospect of relief from Montezuma. It is said that, from one of the towers, the King had looked out upon the conflict in the city. He had marked the fierce spirit of the Spaniards, led on by Cortes, and the desperate resistance of the Mexican troops, headed by his brother, the lord of Iztapalapan. The sight moved him to tears. He felt that his city was in ruins, whoever might be conqueror. Troubled with his distress, after a sleepless night he sought Cortes, and implored him to stop the havoc by leaving the city. It required but little persuasion to bring Cortes to a decision. He promised the King that he would go, if he would insure him a peaceable departure, and, for this purpose, demanded that the Mexicans should lay down their arms: and Montezuma as readily agreed to use his authority to induce them to do so.*

Accordingly, on the next day, when the infuriated Mexicans again attacked the Spanish quarters, Montezuma resolved to show himself to them, hoping thereby to calm their fury. Their attack was now tremendous. It seemed impossible for the artillery to drive them back. Some were scaling the walls, and some had actually forced their way into the quarters, and were fighting hand in hand with the Spaniards, when Montezuma, attired in his regal dress, and attended by some of his nobles and a guard of Spanish soldiers, came out upon the battlements. The moment he appeared, all was silence; some fell reverently upon their knees. The King now spoke to them, beseeching them to desist, and declaring that the Spaniards were ready to leave the city if they would only allow them to pass out undisturbed. One of the nobles answered from the crowd, that

* Bernal Diaz declares that there was no such readiness of agreement between Cortes and Montezuma. His story is, that when Cortes consented to leave the city, desiring, as a condition, that the King should use his influence in inducing his people to lay down their arms, Montezuma instantly refused—bursting into tears, and uttering many reproaches against the Spanish commander. Father Olmedo and Christoval de Olid then tried to persuade the King, but he answered that his remonstrances would produce no effect upon his people: they had chosen another King, and would not allow a single Spaniard to leave the city alive. At length, however, after great difficulty, he was prevailed on to address the Mexicans.

the war would soon be over, for they had all sworn that no Spaniard should leave the city alive. Montezuma again implored them to lay aside their arms, and used every argument to persuade them. All was in vain. A murmur of discontent spread through the throng, and one of the crowd cried out that the King was a coward. In a moment more, the whole mass cursed and reproached him, and then came showers of stones and arrows upon the ramparts. Before the Spaniards could shelter him, Montezuma fell. A stone had struck him on the head, and he was wounded in his arm and leg. The Mexicans were now horror-stricken at their own deed; their stormy passions gave way to gloom and despair; they fled from the spot in dismay.

The Spaniards bore the unfortunate King within, and Cortes caused his wounds to be carefully dressed, and endeavored to console him. But Montezuma refused all comfort. He seemed now as one waking from a dream. The haughty and fierce spirit of his better days came back, and he heaped heavy reproaches upon the Spanish chief. He felt that he was a king; he knew that he was now degraded and disgraced, and he longed to die. In a phrensy, he tore the bandages from his wounds, and refused to take any nourishment whatever. Cortes, perceiving his end approaching, now besought him to embrace the Christian religion. Alas! that Montezuma had so poor a preacher of our blessed religion! Father Olmedo earnestly implored him to receive Christian baptism, but all to no purpose. Unbending to the last, he had but one fixed desire, and that was to die; and at length, after three days of misery, he breathed his last, in a raving passion, mourning over his fate, cursing the Spaniards, and swearing vengeance against his people. Cortes immediately sent a messenger to Prince Cuitlahuatzin, the successor to the throne, to inform him of the death of Montezuma; and in a little time the body was carried out by six nobles, and taken to a place called Copalco, amid the loud lamentations of the Mexicans.

He now endeavored to make peace with the Mexicans, but all his efforts failed. The Indians whom he sent as messengers with his terms refused to return with any answer; but a distinct answer was soon made known by the conduct of the people. The day after the funeral, they returned to their attack upon the Spanish quarters more furiously than ever. The position of Cortes was now well nigh desperate. Montezuma was dead, and there was nothing to restrain the vengeance of the multitude. All hopes of peace had passed away: his only hope was to escape from the city. Even this, however, seemed cut off by the bold determination of the Indians. They had taken possession of a tower on the principal temple, which commanded a full view of the Spanish quarters. From this point they kept so strict a watch, that it was almost certain death to a Spaniard to move out. They knew the advantage of this post so well, that five hundred of their picked warriors were stationed there. Cortes at once saw that it was idle to hope to make his retreat so long as they kept that station. It was absolutely necessary to dislodge them. Accordingly, he sent Escobar out with a strong force for that purpose. More than one gallant effort was made, but at length, after three several failures, Escobar was forced to retreat to the quarters.

Cortes now felt that everything depended upon himself. His men were doomed to perish, unless something could be done. Though suffering from his wound, he determined upon another effort, and resolved to take the command himself. At the head of his troops, he pressed toward the temple. Barriers were placed in his way, stones and arrows were showered upon him; still he pressed on. Unfortunately, when he reached the court of the temple, he found that the cavalry, upon which he principally relied, could not be used; the horses continually slipped, and fell upon the pavement. The Indians annoyed them in every way. Together with their arrows and darts, they hurled upon them burning beams of wood, which threw them into great confusion. Cortes now dismounted, and ordering his men to bind his shield to his wounded arm, rushed to the attack, calling to them to follow him. His example inspired them. The Spaniards rushed on with resistless force. Gradually working their way up the steps, they at length reached the platform, and drove the Mexicans to the upper area of the temple. Here the battle raged furiously for three hours. The priests were there, calling frantically upon the gods, and screaming to the people, and these contested every inch of the way with the desperate Spaniards. The carnage was awful. The warriors were all killed upon the spot, or destroyed themselves by leaping from the tower. The nobles perished to a man. Cortes at last gained the tower, when there was no living being to defend it. He instantly set fire to it, and then commenced his retreat toward his quarters; but his retreat was one continued battle. New multitudes thronged upon him in the lower area; and when these were passed, he met with a furious attack in every street and from every house. Every inch of ground was contested to and from the temple; still in this retreat he managed, by a desperate effort, to rescue his old friend Andres de Duero, whom the Mexicans had seized, and were dragging away for a sacrifice. At length he reached his quarters, every man being covered with blood, and sinking from exhaustion. An uncounted number of the Tlascalans had fallen, forty-six Spaniards had been killed.

and every other Spaniard in the action had been wounded.*

As soon as they had rested from this hard struggle, Cortes summoned his officers, to consult as to the time and manner of their retreat. Some advised that they should sally out boldly by day, when they could see their enemies, and mark every danger. Others thought it best to make the attempt under cover of the night, thinking to escape unobserved through the darkness, and trusting to a superstition of the Mexicans, which would not allow them to attack an enemy during the hours of repose. An old soldier now came in, and pretending to be an astrologer, urged that the attempt should be made by night. In a little time, it was settled that they should start out at midnight. As the Mexicans had broken down the bridges of the

* This spirited attack and defence of the temple was considered of such high importance among the Indians, that it was perpetuated by lively representations in the paintings of both Tlascalans and Mexicans.

Connected with this attack, a beautiful story is told by some historians of the devoted patriotism of two Mexican youths of noble rank. Finding Cortes about to gain the tower, they resolved to sacrifice themselves for the good of their country, by involving in their own death that of the Spanish leader. With this design, they advanced to Cortes, and pretended to kneel down, as if demanding quarter: when suddenly seizing him, they dragged him to the edge of the upper area, resolved to hurl themselves down, and drag him in their fall. Cortes, by a desperate effort, broke from their grasp, and the youths perished in their unsuccessful attempt.

causeways to prevent their escape, Cortes at once caused a portable bridge to be made, strong enough to allow his army and all the baggage to pass the openings. He then commanded all the treasure that had been collected to be brought forward, and separating the fifth part which belonged to the King, left the rest for his men; at the same time advising them not to load themselves with it, as it might prove burdensome in their perilous retreat. He next ordered the plan of march. The van of his army, consisting of two hundred of his best soldiers, together with twenty horsemen, was placed under the command of Sandoval, aided by Diego de Ordaz and Francisco Lugo. The rear, which contained most of the Spanish troops, was intrusted to Pedro de Alvarado and Velasquez de Leon. Cortes himself, aided by Christoval de Olid and Davila, took charge of the centre, in which were placed the children of Montezuma, and other prisoners of distinction, together with the baggage, artillery, and portable bridge. The Tlascalans, Chempoallans, and Cholulans, amounting to several thousands, were scattered among the three divisions. To aid them at the time of their departure, the night set in densely dark, with a thick fog, and heavy falls of rain. At midnight, the van left the quarters, and the other divisions soon followed. In deep silence they moved toward the causeway of Tacuba, because that was known to be the shortest, and least frequented by the Mexicans. They reached the first breach unmolested, and at once commenced fixing their bridge for a passage.

Suddenly the air was filled with the loud yells of the Mexicans. They had watched every movement. The priests sounded their horns, calling their countrymen to battle : the lake was covered with a thousand canoes ; showers of stones and arrows were poured in upon the Spaniards from the boats, while an immense number eagerly thronged the causeway to oppose them. Unfortunately at this time, the bridge broke down under the heavy weight of the baggage and artillery. Some of the Spaniards who had gained the other side hurried to the second breach, while their poor companions struggled to scramble across the horrid chasm, filled up now with one confused heap of baggage, cannon, armor, and the bodies of the dead and dying. All was confusion. The rain fell in torrents ; the horses plunged in every direction ; both sides of the causeway were lined with canoes, from which one continual attack was kept up ; the Spaniards never before had witnessed anything like it. The bellowing of the horses, and the shrieks of the prisoners hurried away for sacrifice, filled the air : all was an indescribable scene of horror. With fury and desperation, many of the Spaniards fought their way over the dreadful gap, and joined their companions at the second breach; while the largest number were either killed on the spot, made prisoners, or drowned. At the second breach, the conflict was the same. It was impossible to preserve any order; friends and foes, soldiers and officers, horse and infantry, men and women, were all struggling there in one wild scene of carnage and horror. By a desperate exertion, Cortes, with some of his hardiest veterans, forced his way across the remaining breaches, " the bodies of the dead serving to fill up the ditches." Having reached the firm land, he left his slender force with Sandoval and Olid, who had managed to escape with him, commanding them to keep in perfect order, to resist any fresh attack, and then plunged back into the fight. His heart would not allow him to leave his men in their deplorable condition. He passed and repassed the last breaches more than once, sometimes swimming, sometimes scrambling over the dead: here he would encourage some sinking man still to fight; there he would pull some drowning man to the firm land, and sometimes drag his captive comrades from the very hands of the enemy. His daring struggles are almost incredible. The sufferings of his men roused every energy; he risked every danger, and wonderful is it that he was not added to the number of the slain. In spite of all his efforts, however, the air still rang with the savage yells of the Mexicans, and the piercing shrieks of the poor captives. It was impossible to rescue all; he did all that man could do; he was heart-sick over his own inability. Now he was joined by a small party, which he found belonged to the rear division. These were Alvarado, bleeding freely, and scarcely able to stand, eight Spaniards, and as many Tlascalans, all wounded and covered with blood. Alvarado declared that these were all that remained of the division intrusted to him: all the rest, officers as well as men, and among them Velasquez de Leon, having been killed or made prisoners; that when he came to the third breach, not being able to face the enemy or to swim across, in an effort of despair he struck his lance in the bottom of the ditch, and leaped to the other side. This effort saved him.*

The dawn of the next day found the Spaniards at Popotla, near Tacuba, and showed them more fully their misery. They lay scattered around at random, wounded, exhausted, and disheartened. More than half the Spaniards had perished, with four thousand of their allies. All the ammunition, artillery, and baggage was lost, together with most of the horses. No treasure whatever was saved;

---

* The place where this happened still goes by the name of "*Salto de Alvarado,*" or Alvarado's Leap; and this dreadful night is still spoken of in New Spain as "*Noche triste,*" or the Night of Sorrow.

those soldiers who had foolishly laden themselves with it having perished for their folly. Well nigh all the Mexican prisoners had likewise perished; among them the prince Cacamatzin, a brother, a son, and two daughters of Montezuma. Velasquez de Leon, Francisco Morla, Francisco Sancedo, and Amador de Lariz, with many other Spanish officers, were missing. The gallant De Leon had been placed in command of the extreme detachment of the rear division, and not even one man of his party was now to be found.

The scene touched the heart of Cortes; he who could brave every danger, overcoming every fear, could not now overcome the feelings of a man. As he looked upon the wretched remnant of his army, and thought of his brave companions who were lost, his heart swelled with sorrow; he sat down upon a stone, and the tears rolled down his face. The death of De Leon was more than he could well bear. He was not only a gallant comrade in arms, but a friend whose heart was ever true to Cortes. But greater disasters were possibly before him; and while this thought added to his misery, it taught him also the necessity of rousing his energies. Alvarado, Sandoval, Olid, Ordaz, Davila, and Lugo, were still around him; his faithful friends Doña Marina, Aguilar, and Father Olmedo, were yet alive. These, with the poor soldiers, were looking to him as their leader, and he felt the necessity of action. The country all around was in arms against him; a shelter from their fury was to be found immediately. He gathered his little force, and made a hurried march to Otoncalpolco, a temple nine miles westward from Mexico. Here parties of the enemy attacked him from time to time through the day, but by watchfulness and courage he managed to drive them back. Still his position was dangerous: if a large party should assault him, he could not resist long. He longed to reach Tlascala, as his only safe resting-place; yet it was far distant, and he knew that the Mexicans were watching to waylay him. He was in great anxiety, hesitating what he should do, when a Tlascalan came forward, and offered to conduct him to his own country by a secret pathway.

CHAPTER VIII.

FOLLOWING their Tlascalan guide, the Spaniards undertook their wearisome march through a desolate country; sometimes struggling through swamps, and then scrambling over mountains. Parties of Mexicans pursued and hung upon their rear, and it required the utmost vigilance and skill to avoid them. Then, too, the region through which they were moving was uninhabited, and destitute of all manner of supplies; they ate gladly such roots and berries as they could find. Arrived at Zacamolco, their famine was so great that they greedily devoured a horse that had been killed that day by the Mexicans. As to the poor Tlascalans, they threw themselves upon the ground, and piteously implored their gods to help them. Cortes bore himself nobly through these sorrows. All eyes were upon him, and his example roused and animated his men. At length, on the sixth day of the march, they came near Otompan. Parties of Mexicans now showed themselves more frequently, and some, as they passed, cried out scornfully, "Advance, advance, robbers, to receive the reward of your crimes!" The valley of Otompan presently burst upon their sight, covered with warriors as far as the eye could reach. Two hundred thousand men, headed by the nobility of the country, had gathered there to oppose them in their march to Tlascala.

The hearts of the Spaniards now sank within them; the stoutest among them were dismayed; their doom was at hand. Cortes was instantly roused; he saw that to allow them to shrink from their danger, was only to increase it. He immediately drew up his wretched army, and flanking it on each side with the few horsemen he could still command, cried out with enthusiasm, "The moment is arrived when we must either conquer or perish! Castilians, rouse your spirits, place your confidence on high, and advance boldly to the charge!" With this, he rushed to the conflict. The Indians fought with the fury of revenge, the Spaniards with the fury of despair. More than once the brave band of Cortes broke through the lines of the enemy, but new multitudes thronged upon them instantly. They were overpowered with numbers. For four hours this horrid fight continued. Cortes perceived his men falling fast, some dead, and others dying; all seemed well nigh lost. A bold thought now struck him. He remembered to have heard that the Mexicans were always routed when their general was slain and their standard taken. He determined to make one last effort. Cihuacatzin, the leader of the Indians, was in the midst of his troops, sitting upon his litter, surrounded by a guard; and the standard, fastened to his back, was floating over his head. Cortes, calling to Alvarado, Sandoval, Olid, and Davila, to follow him close and guard him from attack, dashed toward the general. With a desperate fury he broke through the crowd, reached the centre of the army, and with one blow of his lance laid Cihuacatzin on the ground. One of the brave Spaniards who followed leaped from his horse, tore the standard from the general, and instantly despatched him. In a moment, the enemy was in confusion; the hopes of the Spaniards revived: they pressed hard upon them, routed and pursued them. They gained their victory, however, at a great sacrifice. Numbers of the Spaniards and Tlascalans were slain, and every survivor carried his wounds. Cortes himself was dangerously wounded by a blow on the head. Yet the conquerors left dead upon that field twenty thousand of the enemy.*

* It is said that in this battle, a woman, called Maria de Estrada, particularly distinguished herself. With her lance and shield, she was seen in the midst of the conflict, bearing herself with extraordinary courage.

With the remnant of his army (only four hundred and forty men), Cortes now marched without further trouble into the Tlascalan territories. Here he was received with great kindness; indeed, the kindness of the Tlascalans increased with his misfortunes. They ministered in every way to the comfort of his feeble but victorious army. But, unfortunately, some of his own men began once more to trouble him. Wearied with their continual hardships, the soldiers of Narvaez returned to their murmurs; and, strange to tell, among these murmurers was Andres de Duero, the friend of Cortes. The discontent increased; the disaffected held meetings from time to time, and at last signed and sent a remonstrance to Cortes, urging him to abandon the country and return to Cuba.

Cortes received this with great self-possession, but in deep sorrow. His spirit was unbroken by his trials; though misfortune had followed him, he still carried in his heart the fixed resolution of conquering Mexico. With such a determination, he could not well part with any of his men. The best mode of silencing their murmurs was to keep them busy, and he soon found employment for them. The people of Tepejacac had sworn alliance to Cortes, but in the midst of his misfortunes had treacherously taken up arms against the Spaniards, and cut off a body of his countrymen on their march from Chempoalla to Mexico. Cortes resolved to punish them for this conduct. With much difficulty, he persuaded his men to join him in this effort, the followers of Narvaez at length assenting, because the Spaniards that had been slaughtered belonged to their party. At the head of four thousand Tlascalans, together with his men, he now set out for these people.

He soon subdued the Tepejacacans, penetrating even to their principal town. This region being fertile, and directly on the road to Villa Rica, he established in it a settlement, which he called *Segura de la Frontera.* Intent upon keeping his men employed, he continued his marches now in various directions. For months he pursued this line of conduct, meeting with success in almost every engagement. These little advantages, though slight, cheered him in the thought of conquering Mexico. He would not abandon that idea. Indeed, his resolution on this point was so fixed, that he had already ordered a quantity of timber to be cut in the forests of Tlascala for the construction of twelve brigantines, that he might get command of the lake; and Martin Lopez, an experienced shipwright, was now busy at this work. What he most needed was an addition to his numbers; with his little force, he could hardly hope to achieve that conquest. Fortune now smiled on him. Diego Velasquez, ignorant of the fate of Narvaez, sent Pedro Barba with a small company to the country, bearing letters to Narvaez. These letters brought positive orders to Narvaez to send Cortes, if alive, to Cuba that he might be taken thence in fetters to Spain; such being the command of the Bishop of Burgos.* Barba and his followers were artfully decoyed on shore by the men at Villa Rica, seized, and sent prisoners to Cortes. The Spanish chief, with his usual policy, received them as friends and countrymen, and soon persuaded them to join his enterprise. Barba now informed him that another vessel would soon appear off the coast, laden with supplies. By good management, the crew and cargo of this vessel were also secured. In a little time, a much larger reinforcement was added to him. The party sent out under Pineda, by Garay, the Governor of Jamaica, to establish a settlement at Panuco, had all been destroyed; and the Governor, ignorant of this fact, now sent another body, under Camarjo, to aid Pineda in his labors. This second party, learning the fate of their countrymen, and being at the same time afflicted with the diseases of the country, sought refuge in the settlement at Vera Cruz. Thence they proceeded to Frontera, found Cortes, and at once entered his service. Other bodies sent out by Garay, for the same purpose of aiding the colony at Panuco, followed their example;

* The Bishop of Burgos had the principal charge of West India affairs in Spain. He was a warm friend to the Governor of Cuba, and, of course, an enemy to Cortes.

and Cortes soon found, to his great joy, that he had added to his numbers very unexpectedly one hundred and eighty men and twenty horses. His hopes for the conquest were now brightening.

To his sorrow, however, the followers of Narvaez again returned to their murmurs. They urged more earnestly than ever that they ought to be sent back to Cuba. Cortes perceived that the spirit of discontent was growing, and felt that it was better to lose these men, than to allow them to remain any longer, spreading dissatisfaction in his army. Accordingly, he issued his proclamation, stating that all those who wished to return to Cuba might do so, and that a safe passage should be immediately furnished for them. Some of the discontented were now ashamed, and determined to remain; but the larger part resolved to start, and among these was Andres de Duero. Cortes selected one of the best vessels that had belonged to Narvaez, and allowed them to embark. At the same time he sent Diego de Ordaz and Alonzo de Mendoza to Spain, to represent his conduct, and keep an eye on the Bishop of Burgos. Alonzo Davila was also sent to Hispaniola, to tell of their hardships and sufferings, the jealousy of Velasquez, and the cruelty of the Bishop of Burgos, and beg assistance for the enterprise; while another officer was despatched to Jamaica, with power to enlist soldiers, and purchase horses and supplies.

Having despatched these, he hurried his preparations for the siege of Mexico. The timber for his ships being nearly ready, and the cordage, cables, sails, and other rigging, brought over from Villa Rica, he saw nothing to delay his march toward the capital. He called his officers together, and, after consultation, it was determined to make their head-quarters at Tezcuco, as that seemed the place best adapted for annoying the enemy. Messages were now sent to the confederate Indians, to hold themselves in readiness at any moment, and the troops were reviewed. Cortes found that he still had five hundred and fifty infantry, among whom were eighty musketeers and crossbow-men, and nine pieces of artillery. Besides these, there were forty horsemen: and to the whole he added an army of ten thousand Tlascalans. This was his force for the conquest of Mexico. On the 28th of December (six months after his fatal retreat), he moved again toward the capital.

Mexico was now in a far different condition from that in which Cortes left it. The six months that had passed away had been improved by its citizens. Cuitlahuitzin, the successor of Montezuma, had not only distinguished himself by his bold attack upon the Spaniards on the night of their retreat, but he had repaired the damages done to his city by the invaders, made fortifications, and filled the magazines with armor. With all this he had, if possible, infused into his countrymen a still more deadly hatred of the Spaniards. But in the midst of these labors, he had been cut down by the small pox,* and now Guatimozin, the nephew of Montezuma, ruled over the kingdom. He was a very young man, but had exhibited such daring courage and great ability, that the people had called him to the throne.

At the end of three days, without any opposition, Cortes entered Tezcuco. The streets were completely deserted; neither men, women, nor children, were to be seen. The people had carried their goods to the forests, or the borders of the lake, while the lord of Tezcuco and the nobles had fled to Mexico. Cortes soon learned that Tezcuco was divided into two parties, and instantly took advantage of it. The prince who had fled was said to be an usurper, who had murdered his elder brother, and his usurpation had been aided by the King of Mexico. At the same time a youth was pointed out to Cortes as the lawful heir, and he immediately caused him to be proclaimed lord of Tezcuco. He succeeded in persuading this youth to embrace Christianity, and at his baptism he received the name of Hernan Cortes, the Spanish chief standing as the godfather. Cortes then appointed Escobar and two other Spaniards to attend

---

* The small pox had been introduced into the kingdom by a slave who came into the country with Narvaez.

upon the new lord. Terms of friendship were at once made : the young man engaging to do all in his power to aid the Spaniards ; which engagement, it is said, he kept religiously.

Having thus arranged matters at Tezcuco, remembering certain acts of Cuitlahuitzin, the former lord of Iztapalapan, he determined to attack that city. Accordingly, at the head of two hundred and thirty-five Spaniards and all the Tlascalan army, he marched against it. At their approach, all the inhabitants fled to their canoes. The Spaniards took possession without any trouble, and as the night was coming on, resolved to make their quarters there. They had scarcely retired, when the water began to rise and overflow the city. The Iztapalapans had broken the mole of the lake, hoping to drown them. The Tezcucans gave the alarm in time, and, with great difficulty, Cortes made good his retreat. He lost, however, two of his men, a number of Tlascalans, and one of the horses. This ingenuity of the Indians troubled him very much ; he felt that his enemies were more dangerous than he had supposed them to be.

His next effort was to get possession of the two towns of Chalco and Tlalmamalco, places of great importance to the Spaniards, as they lay directly between Tlascala and Tezcuco. Accordingly, Sandoval and Lugo were sent with a body of two hundred men to drive the Mexicans from them.

This they easily accomplished. Messengers now came from Mizquic, Otompan, and other cities, begging the protection of the Spaniards; all of whom Cortes received very kindly, readily making terms with them.

All the materials for building his vessels being at length ready, Cortes determined to have them brought from Tlascala to Tezcuco. This was an important business, and Sandoval was selected to perform it. On the way to Tlascala was the town of Zoltepec, whose inhabitants (at the time when Cortes was hurrying to the relief of Alvarado) had surprised and murdered forty Spaniards and three hundred Tlascalans, on their march from Vera Cruz to Mexico. Cortes was resolved to punish them for this act, and consequently gave orders to Sandoval to stop there and chastise them on his way. When Sandoval approached this city, the inhabitants fled. He pursued them, and made many prisoners. The piteous cries of the women, however, induced him to spare them all; they expressed great sorrow for what they had done, and he only exacted from them a promise of obedience and good conduct for the future. This was the more generous in the leader, inasmuch as he discovered many things to rouse his revenge. In one of the temples, he saw the walls and idols besmeared with the blood of his countrymen; while the skins of two of their faces, together with those of four horses, were hung upon the altars. On a wall in one of the houses he found this inscription: "In this place Juan Zuste and his wretched companions were confined." From Zoltepec, Sandoval moved on to Tlascala, where he found all ready, and Chichimecatl, with a large army of Tlascalans, prepared to start. Eight thousand men were employed in carrying the timbers, cordage, and other materials. A Spanish guard went before them, and a guard of allies was placed on each side. In this mode they marched out from Tlascala. Flying parties of Indians sometimes were seen, but none dared to approach them. At length they came near to Tezcuco. Great was the joy now of the Spaniards in that city. Cortes and his officers came out to meet the procession, and the Spanish leader, with great delight, embraced Chichimecatl and two other chiefs, and thanked them for their great kindness. Six hours were spent in entering Tezcuco. It was a perfect jubilee. The allies, dressed in their finest garments, and decked off with their gay plumes, marched through the streets, sounding their horns and beating their drums, while the air rang with the shouts of triumph for Castile and Tlascala.

Martin Lopez, the shipwright, now declared that it required twenty days to make ready for the launching, and Cortes determined to keep his men employed in the mean time in reducing the cities that were friendly to Guatimozin. Leaving Sandoval at Tezcuco, with a party of his followers he attacked the cities of Xaltocan and Tacubs, the first of which was plundered and partly destroyed by fire. Upon his return, Sandoval sallied out and routed their enemies at Huaxtepec and Jacapitchtla. To add to their joy at this time, a further reinforcement of Spaniards arrived at Tezcuco, under Julian de Alderete. Alderete stated that the vessel which had brought him was now lying at Vera Cruz, laden with military stores for the army, and (what was still better news for Cortes) that the Bishop of Burgos, one of his principal enemies, had been deposed from his authority over the West Indies.

Motives of policy, as well as the desire to preserve the city of Mexico (for Cortes felt assured now that he should conquer it), prompted the Spanish leader to send messengers to Guatimozin, proposing to make terms of peace. Guatimozin, however, would listen to no terms; he sent back a scornful answer, and Cortes at once returned to his depredations. The city of Quauhnahuac was next attacked and reduced. Thence he sallied against Xochimilco, a large town on the lake of Chalco. Here multitudes had gathered to oppose him; they had cut down the bridges to stop him, and erected palisades to shelter themselves. The eager Spaniards dashed into the stream, and many lost their lives in attempting to swim over. The battle was fierce on both sides. In this struggle Cortes came near losing his life. His horse fell under him, while surrounded by the enemy: he was instantly knocked down; a crowd seized him and were carrying him off in triumph. At this moment, Christoval de Olid, perceiving his perilous condition, dashed forward with a body of Tlascalans, and, by a mighty effort, rescued him. Cortes and Olid both received dangerous wounds on the head. Many of his soldiers being also wounded, he was forced to remain four days at this place, that they might all recruit. During this time, the enemy annoyed them very much. A party of four of his men having wandered off to sack a house on the shore of the lake, the Mexicans came in canoes, surrounded it, and carried them off. These unfortunate captives were taken to Guatimozin, who examined them very particularly as to the numbers that followed Cortes. After gaining from them all the information he could, he ordered their hands and feet to be cut off. In this condition they were exhibited through the country, until at length he commanded that they should be killed.

To his surprise, Cortes discovered now that some of his men were still disaffected; indeed, that this disaffection had even ripened into a plot to destroy him. The few remaining soldiers of Narvaez were once more the cause of the trouble. The principal man among them was Antonio Villafaña. He was still a warm friend to Velasquez, and, of course, disliked the Spanish leader. Though a private soldier, he was a man of uncommon power; energetic, resolute, and persuasive, he secretly cherished discontent among the men with great success. From time to time they met at his quarters, until at length, having prepared them for action, he boldly proposed that they should murder Cortes and his principal officers, give the command of the army to a brother-in-law of Velasquez, and force him to take them back to Cuba. They all welcomed the proposition, bound themselves by an oath, and signed their names to a paper presented by Villafaña. Their plan was to murder them while at table: a letter, feigned to have come from Vera Cruz, was to be presented to Cortes, and while he was engaged in reading it, the fatal blow was to be given. Others soon joined them; they felt strong; the day was fixed. On the eve of that day, a soldier (one of the original followers of Cortes) came to the commander, and begged that he might see him privately. His request was immediately granted. He now threw himself at the feet of Cortes, unfolded the whole plan, and implored his forgiveness; he was one of the conspirators, but had not the heart to be so longer. The news startled Cortes; yet he was, as usual, self-possessed. He instantly summoned Sandoval, Alvarado, and some others of the intended victims, and proceeded to Villafaña's quarters. Numbers were there; they were taken by surprise; they looked like guilty men. Some tried to escape, but were immediately taken. Cortes himself seized Villafaña, and snatched from his bosom the paper containing the names of the conspirators. The accomplices of Villafaña were carried to prison, while he was immediately brought to trial. His guilt was proved, he was condemned to die, and the next morning was seen hanging before the door of his quarters.

The paper showed names surprising to Cortes: the conspiracy was far deeper than he had supposed. It was impossible, however, to bring these men to execution; he could not spare them. With great presence of mind, he ordered the prisoners to be set at liberty, and then assembled all his troops. He now told them of the awful plot that had threatened destruction to all their hopes. Pointing to the body of Villafaña, he called on them to look upon the traitor, declaring that he was very happy that his doom fell upon no other Spaniard; that there were other conspirators, but he was ignorant as to who they were; he himself had arrested Villafaña, but in his confusion and fright the guilty man had swallowed a paper containing the names of his accomplices; and who these accomplices might be, could now never be known. The guilty men in the crowd were at once relieved; they fancied they were unsuspected, while at the same time their leader knew them all, and watched them closely.

In a little time, they were gathered together on a more joyous occasion. Martin Lopez had worked diligently, and all was now ready for the launch. The Spaniards having attended mass and received the communion, the whole army was drawn up on the banks of the canal. The brigantines glided gently into the water, while Father Olmedo stood by to bless them and give their names. The sails were then hoisted, to try them; and, as they ploughed the water, the "*te Deum*" was chanted, while the words echoed with the roar of artillery and shouts of joy.

CHAPTER IX.

CORTES reviewed his army once more, preparatory to his attack upon the city of Mexico. He found that he had eighty-six horsemen, eight hundred infantry, together with three large cannons, fifteen small field-pieces, a thousand pounds of gunpowder, and a large quantity of balls and arrows. To these he added an immense number of Tlascalans and other allies, and then divided his army into three parts, placing over these his well-tried officers Sandoval, Alvarado, and Olid. The towns of Tepejacac, Tacuba, and Cojohuacan, were situated on the causeways, and served to guard the city from the first attacks. The three divisions were to take possession of these three places, while Cortes himself took the command of the fleet, which was considered the most important part of the enterprise.

The parties soon set out for their respective

positions. Alvarado and Olid in a little time reached Tacuba. The aqueduct of Chapoltepec passed through this place, affording a supply of fresh water to the Mexican capital. This they determined to destroy, and at once set to the work. The Mexicans opposed them fiercely; the struggle was a hard one, but at length they succeeded in cutting off the pipes. Flushed with success, they now attempted to take possession of the first bridge on the causeway of Tacuba. As they approached this spot, they found immense numbers gathered to oppose them; the causeway was thronged with the enemy, while each side was lined with canoes, from which the Mexicans poured in their arrows. At the first discharge, three Spaniards were slain, and thirty wounded. The Spaniards only fought the more fiercely; yet, after all their efforts, they were forced to retreat to Tacuba, eight of their number being dead, and more than fifty wounded. Leaving Alvarado, Olid pushed on to his station at Cojohuacan.

In the mean time, Cortes had brought the fleet out on the lake, and after various manœuvres, proceeded to attack a rock near the city, where a large number of the inhabitants had fled for refuge The Mexicans, perceiving his design, sent out their whole naval force (consisting of four thousand canoes) against his brigantines. Cortes now moved fairly out into the lake, and formed his fleet in the shape of a crescent to receive them. As they came near, the sails of the brigantines were spread, and they dashed through them, overturning some, and scattering the rest, to the great loss of the Mexicans. Olid had now reached his post, and from the temple at Cojohuacan saw the conflict on the lake. He instantly pushed along the causeway toward the city, drove the Mexicans from some of the trenches, and took possession. Cortes now attacked the bastion called Xoloc, situated at the angle made by the junction of the roads of Cojohuacan and Iztapalapan. The Mexicans defended the place with great obstinacy; multitudes fell in their efforts to save it, but it was stormed and taken. As this was a spot of great importance, and in direct communication with the division of Olid, Cortes determined to establish his camp here. The three divisions were now on the three causeways, and, as the principal attacks of the enemy were from the canoes that lined them, he distributed his fleet so as to protect the three divisions in their three efforts against the city—giving orders that they were to be managed in strict obedience to the three officers in command. The siege now regularly commenced.

From this moment, a series of attacks, retreats, skirmishes, and manœuvres, were going on upon the causeways. The causeway of Tacuba was the shortest, and it was supposed that Alvarado would be the first, therefore, to enter the city. But the fact that it was the shortest caused it to be the most carefully guarded. Every morning, Alvarado renewed his attempt, and each day met with a sharp opposition. At night, the Mexicans repaired whatever damage he had done, and in the morning showed themselves as stubborn as ever; while the Spaniards, regardless of wounds, endeavored to push their way onward to the capital, and were continually disappointed in their hope of reaching it. Alvarado perceived now, to his sorrow, that the destruction of the aqueduct of Chapoltepec had not taken from the city its supply of water. Canoes were seen continually by night bringing casks from the towns on the borders of the lake. Provisions were brought in the same way; thus defeating the hope of reducing the city by famine. Two of the brigantines were set to watch these boats and intercept them, but the cunning of the Mexicans defeated this. Their canoes were sailing in every direction, to beguile them. So far from being taken themselves, they even contrived to tempt the two brigantines near the border of the lake, where thirty of their largest boats lay in ambush. An attack was instantly made: the brigantines could not well be worked in that position; every Spaniard was wounded, and one of the captains killed. To increase the difficulty of the siege, periodical rains now set in; these, however, did not deter Alvarado and his followers from their attempts, though these attempts were still unsuccessful. Whatever advance he made, however, was a safe one; if he gained a foot of ground, he kept it Houses were destroyed and ditches filled behind him as far as he passed, to enable him to make good his retreat, if it became necessary. Very much the same scenes were passing on the other causeways. Daily efforts were made, both by land and water, to force an entrance into the city, and all proved unsuccessful.

At last, wearied and mortified with continued disappointment, Cortes resolved upon a general assault. Accordingly, he commanded Alvarado and Sandoval to lead on their divisions, regardless of all opposition, while he himself took the command of the division at Cojohuacan. The order was instantly obeyed: the three divisions moved forward. The Mexicans met them with the fury of madmen; their opposition was tremendous. In spite of this opposition, however, Cortes continued to gain ground, carrying everything before him. Julian de Alderete, according to command that he should follow on and fill up all ditches behind him, was close upon him, but, in the ardor of the struggle, neglected this necessary duty. The Mexicans at length fled before Cortes, in apparent dismay, and he reached the capital. This was only a stratagem: the design was to bring him beyond the narrow pass in the causeway. He had no sooner entered the city, than the big drum was struck, the horns in the temple sent forth their blasts: the Mexicans raised their horrid yells, and at once flocked to the causeway. Alarmed for the safety of his men, Cortes ordered a retreat. Accordingly, they commenced retreating, but when they reached the narrow pass, all was confusion. Multitudes pressed upon them by land, arrows were showered upon them from the boats; it was now a general rout. Struggling to escape, the men pushed on only to plunge into the big ditch left open by Alderete. In that fatal gap fell men and horses, Spaniards and Indians, all in one mighty struggle. Cortes was still self-possessed; regardless of his life, he plunged into the gap, animating some, and rescuing others. Many a sinking companion did he save that day. In the midst of these noble struggles, he received a wound in the leg; six Mexicans seized him, and were carrying him off in triumph. At this critical moment, two brave Spaniards, Olea and Lerma, rushed to his rescue. Olea killed four of the Mexicans, and then lost his own life; while Lerma, sinking with his wounds, would likewise have been a captive, had not Quinones, with a body of Spaniards and Tlascalans, at that instant snatched them from their danger. Cortes was lifted out of the water and placed upon a horse; the miserable remnant of his division escaping as it could.

Alvarado was hardly more successful. Having vanquished Cortes, the enemy now rushed upon him in greater numbers. To aid them, they cunningly threw into his ranks five bleeding heads, swearing that they were the heads of Cortes, Sandoval, and other chiefs, and that Alvarado's should soon be added to the number. The Spaniards were in dismay; they supposed that their brave leader had perished, and could fight no longer. Alvarado ordered a hasty retreat, and with great difficulty escaped with a part of his division.

The division of Sandoval suffered the least loss. He had pressed far on toward the city, and felt sure of success, when suddenly numbers rushed upon him, both Cortes and Alvarado being defeated. The Mexicans resorted to the same stratagem that had been practised upon Alvarado. With desperate energy, however, he continued the fight, until, finding that there was no hope of success, he commenced retreating. By an effort of skill, he managed his retreat in so orderly a manner, that only two of his men were killed. The great mass, however (among them Sandoval himself), was wounded. In this general assault, which had thus ended, sixty Spaniards and a great number of allies were slain, while almost every survivor was suffering from his wounds. In addition to this, they lost six horses, one cannon, and a quantity of their arms

Night now closed in, but not to give them rest. The Mexicans prepared for a frightful festival. The Spaniards heard the sound of the big drum, and the blasts of the horns and trumpets, mingled with the exulting yells of the conquerors, while in the temples, that were brilliantly illuminated, they saw the priests moving about, and their poor captive comrades made to dance naked before the idols. Then, too, they could hear the piercing shrieks of the wretched prisoners as they were laid upon the altars to be sacrificed; and while they spent the long night weeping for their friends, they vowed in their hearts an awful revenge.

After this defeat, the Mexicans sent the heads of those slain in sacrifice to all the neighboring towns and provinces, declaring to the people that the gods, being delighted with the blood of those sacrifices, had promised that in eight days the hated Spaniards should all be destroyed, and peace restored to their empire. This was a cunning stratagem. The superstition of the Indians allowed them to believe the story; and thus those provinces already hostile to the Spaniards, became more bitter in their hatred, while their allies began to desert. Even the Tlascalans were disposed to abandon him.* Cortes very prudently determined to attempt nothing during these eight

* It is said that Chichimecatl, the young lord of Tezcuco, and eight Tlascalans, were all that stood by him.

days. He placed himself on the defensive, and resolved to wait quietly until the Indians should see that the story was idle.

Eight days passed away, and the Spaniards were still undestroyed. The Indians now flocked again to the standard of Cortes in larger numbers than ever; he soon had the command of fifty thousand allies. Just at this time, a vessel arrived at Villa Rica with men and ammunition. This last article was very much needed, as the Spaniards had spent nearly all their gunpowder. With a heart unbroken by his fresh calamity, and still carrying the fixed determination of conquering Mexico, Cortes now resolved upon another attack. This time he was resolved to trust to prudence as well as courage; and, giving up all thought of preserving the city, he at once commenced his siege of destruction.

The three divisions were commanded to advance in strict military order: they were to destroy every house in the way; while the allies, following immediately behind, were to fill up all ditches—thereby making a retreat easy, if necessary. The divisions started, and the plan was regularly followed up. Day after day the Mexicans found themselves shut up in narrower limits; yet Guatimozin continued his resistance, and seemed determined to see the last house in Mexico razed to the ground before he would consent that the Spaniards should enter the city. At length, Alvarado with his division worked his way to the great square of Tlalteloco. He found that a great number of warriors and priests had gathered in the temple which commanded the entrance to the square; and as his comrades from the other causeways were to meet in this square (the general mustering-place agreed upon), he determined to attack them. With his whole force, he rushed impetuously forward, gained the temple, drove out the Mexicans, set fire to the idols, and planted the Spanish banner on the top of the building, to cheer his approaching companions.

This was a joyous signal to Cortes and Sandoval. With renewed energies they pressed on, and in four days joined Alvarado in the square. His plan was thus far successful; he was now master of the western portion of the city, and Cortes resolved to pursue it further. Before doing this, however, he sent another messenger to Guatimozin with proposals. The proud Mexican King again gave him a scornful answer, and the Spaniards at once renewed their operations. Every day the Mexicans were enclosed in a narrower compass, while a heap of ruins continued to mark the progress of the Spaniards. The situation of the Mexicans was now awful. The brigantines commanded the lake, the Tlascalans cut off all communication by land; and thus the horrors of famine were added to those of war. The want of food soon produced disease among them, and now the awful horrors of war, famine, and pestilence, were all upon them. Every night the poor famishing creatures were prowling about the Spanish quarters in search of food; every day they were shut up in smaller limits. The heart of Guatimozin was touched, but not subdued; with a proud and unconquerable spirit, he seemed resolved to see his beautiful capital one complete ruin, rather than submit. All the city, except one small quarter, was now in possession of the Spaniards, and this was soon to share the fate of the rest.

The command of the fleet was given to Sandoval. He was to attack that quarter by sea, while Cortes made an assault by land. The Mexicans now perceived that all was well nigh over, and tried to persuade Guatimozin to quit the place, fly to the distant provinces, and there rally his troops. To aid him in this matter, they brought to Cortes pretended proposals of peace—hoping that while he was negotiating with them, Guatimozin might escape. In this plan they were disappointed: the bold defence of Guatimozin, with his bold answers, had taught the Spanish chief that the death or captivity of that prince was necessary to the establishment of the Spaniards in his kingdom. Determined, therefore, that he should in no way escape, he had given strict commands to Sandoval to be on the lookout. Every canoe was closely watched. Seeing some large boats moving speedily toward the land, Sandoval gave signal for a chase. Garcia Holguin, who commanded the swiftest brigantine, soon came up with them. From the superior appearance of one of the boats, he judged it to be the King's, and instantly prepared to fire upon it. Guatimozin now showed himself, and declared he was ready to submit. With the Queen and his attendants he was immediately taken on board the vessel. His first demand was that he might be taken before the Spanish general. He was carried to the shore, and brought before Cortes. Though vanquished, his spirit was unbroken. He cried out to the Spaniard, "*Malinatzin*, I have done all in my power to defend my kingdom and my people. All my efforts have been fruitless. I have nothing else to attempt. Take your dagger and stab me to the heart!" Cortes was too much of a soldier not to feel. Guatimozin was a young man (only then five-and-twenty), and, though a captive, had proved himself a hero. He endeavored to console him in his sorrow, promising that he should continue to reign, subject to the authority of the King of Spain; and commanded that he, with his family, should be treated with marked respect. The siege was now ended: he was master of the capital.

But what was the capital now? Three fourths

of that once beautiful city lay in ruins, and all the squares, streets, and courts, were filled with dead bodies. It was scarcely possible to move without stumbling over them. Bernal Diaz (one of the soldiers of Cortes) declares that "all the streets, squares, and houses, were covered with the bodies of the slain; among the heaps of which were to be seen many wretches crawling about in an advanced stage of those loathsome diseases produced by famine, or unnatural food, exhaustion, and infected air. The trees had been stripped of their bark—the earth dug up, in search of food. Not a drop of fresh water could be found." The Spaniards had lost in that siege more than one hundred of their men; their allies had lost thousands; while no less than one hundred and fifty thousand Mexicans had perished. The air was polluted with the masses of the dead. Cortes was forced to leave the city, that it might be cleansed; and during three days and nights the causeways were filled with miserable beings carrying off the dead.*

In all this misery, the Spaniards felt the joy of conquerors. They had endured a hard struggle; their enemy was subdued: they were now to find their treasures. Returning to the city, they commenced their search; but it was only to be disappointed. No booty was to be gathered; the whole

* It is said that Maria Estrada again distinguished herself in this siege, together with Beatriz Bermudez, and several other women.

quantity of gold that was discovered amounted only to one hundred and twenty thousand dollars, hardly sufficient to pay the expense of the enterprise. Their golden hopes were clouded: now they began to murmur. By the advice of Father Olmedo, this treasure was divided among the sick and wounded. The murmurs of the discontented now became louder; they began to insinuate that Cortes was unjust. There was a rumor that Guatimozin, four days before he was taken, had thrown quantities of gold and precious stones into the lake, to disappoint the avarice of the Spaniards; and now they openly declared that Cortes knew more about this matter than he was willing to confess. They demanded that Guatimozin should be put to the torture until he should confess where the treasures were hid. Cortes very properly refused this cruel demand. They were only the more clamorous, crying out that it was no good feeling which prompted him to deny them, but a desire to keep the place concealed, that he alone might have all the treasure. A revolt was openly talked of. Thus ungenerously accused, to prove his innocence, in a weak moment Cortes allowed them to seize Guatimozin. He was instantly put to the torture. The agony was borne by the unfortunate King with unflinching fortitude, until Cortes, in a rage, snatched him away from them. He had no story to tell: the treasures were not to be found.* The life of this unhappy captive was, however, only prolonged three years; the statement of a Mexican inducing the Spaniards to suspect a revolt, in which he was said to be concerned, he was condemned to die, and was hanged.

Cortes now resolved to send some of his men to the distant provinces, to subdue them and plant settlements. This was necessary, to make his conquest complete; while, at the same time, it would serve to employ his soldiers, turn their thoughts from their disappointment, and possibly lead them to the treasures they desired. Accordingly, Sandoval, Olid, and others, were started off with parties in various directions.

But while he was thus busily engaged in conquests which were daily adding kingdoms to the Spanish crown, his enemies had been busy in Spain. The Bishop of Burgos and others tormented the King with the entreaty to take all power and command from the Spanish conqueror. Moved by their importunities, Charles at last consented. Mexico was scarcely reduced, when Christoval de Tapia arrived at Vera Cruz, with full

* There is a story that the lord of Tacuba was put to the torture with Guatimozin. The mode of torture was, by anointing their feet with oil, and exposing them to fire. This poor man, it is said, died in the midst of it, and in his last agony cast an imploring look toward the King. Guatimozin, observing this look, cried out reproachfully, "Am I reposing on a bed of roses?"

power to seize Cortes, and treat him as a guilty man. Alvarado, who was in command at Villa Rica, received Tapia very kindly, but at the same time sent a messenger to Cortes, to tell him of the danger that threatened him. Tapia was now advancing toward Mexico, and Cortes commanded some of his officers to go out and meet him, that they might come to terms peaceably. Father Olmedo and others persuaded him to return to Chempoalla, and there show his commission to them. Tapia was treated with great respect, but he soon found that he was dealing with men more cunning than himself, and that he could hardly hope to fulfil his orders; time was wasted, and his business not at all forwarded. By the advice of his friends, Cortes now tried the power of gold upon Tapia. The plan succeeded; he was at once bought over.

This danger being averted, Cortes now set diligently to the work of rebuilding Mexico. This was to be done in grand style, suitable to the capital of the New World. The ruins and rubbish being cleared away, grounds were marked off for the erection of churches, convents, and public buildings, while others were laid out for squares and market-places. He caused a magnificent palace to be erected for himself, and here took up his residence. His old prisoner Narvaez was now thought of. Sending to Villa Rica, he had him brought to Mexico, that he might be reconciled to him. Cortes received him with great kindness, embraced him warmly, and would not allow him to submit to the custom of kissing his hand. He was now at liberty. This generosity was forgotten by Narvaez. Led on by the Bishop of Burgos, he became afterward one of the bitterest enemies of Cortes.

15*

CHAPTER X.

WHILE thus employed at the capital, Cortes was suddenly called off by a revolt in the province of Panuco. The natives of that region had risen in arms, and massacred many of the Spaniards who had gone there to make settlements. Cortes instantly, upon hearing this, marched out against them, routed them in two battles, forced them to submit to his authority, and then returned to Mexico to continue his labors.

As past experience had taught him to dread the influence of his enemies in Spain, he determined to send messengers once more to that kingdom, to watch his interests and represent his conduct. Accordingly, two of his particular friends, Alonzo Davila and Quiñones, were despatched there, bearing a rich present of gold and jewels to the King, together with a request from their countrymen that the chief command of New Spain might be given to their leader. At the same time, Cortes sent letters, to advance his own interests and those of his faithful officers. These messengers were very unfortunate on their voyage. Quiñones was killed in a duel at Terceira, and Davila was made a prisoner by a French privateer and carried to France. From this point, however, he was enabled to send his letters to Don Martin, the father of Hernan Cortes. The apprehensions of Cortes were well founded. A furious contest was now going on in Spain about him. All manner of charges were brought against him by the Bishop of Burgos, backed by Narvaez and Tapia, who had now returned to Spain; while his cause was strongly supported by his father Don Martin, and his officers Francisco de Montejo and Diego de Ordaz. Fortunately, these last succeeded in gaining the friendship of the Duke of Bejar and other powerful grandees; and now the claims of the conqueror were so ably sustained before the King, that justice forced him to yield. Cortes had conquered the new kingdom; Cortes could rule it; and to him, therefore, was now sent out a commission as " Captain-General and Governor of New Spain." At the same time, a number of men were despatched by the King to collect and manage the royal revenues.

Upon receiving this commission, Cortes continued to carry out his plans most vigorously. The city of Mexico was hourly rising from its ruins, while his officers, despatched in every direction, were wandering through the distant provinces, searching for mines, or making settlements. So devoted were his followers now, that it is said he might, without an effort, have become an absolute monarch over the new region he had conquered. But his heart was true to his king; he desired no such honor. It was enough for him to have added so vast an empire to the land of his birth, and now to rule over it under the authority of another.

About this time, Garay, the Governor of Jamaica, set sail, with a large body of followers, for the reduction of Panuco. At Cuba he heard of the great exploits of Cortes, and that this province was subdued by him. Having, however, his commission from the Bishop of Burgos, he hoped to negotiate with Cortes, and assume the command: and therefore continued his voyage. The weather driving him into the river Palmas, he landed his men, and determined to march into Panuco. Upon reaching that place, he found that the soldiers of Cortes had possession; his own soldiers began to join them, and he saw that his adventure was an idle one. Vallejo, who commanded the settlement of San Estevan, had sent notice of his arrival to Cortes; and Alvarado, Sandoval, and Father Olmedo, were sent to Panuco, with commands for Garay to leave the country. But Garay's position was hardly that of an opponent; a large number of his men had deserted him, and he was forced to request Cortes to aid him in making them return to their duty. They were soon on terms of peace; and, at the suggestion of Father Olmedo, the Governor's son was married to Doña Catalina, the daughter of Cortes.

The expedition of Garay, however, gave trouble in another way. His soldiers went to wandering through the country, insulting and robbing the natives, until at last they became exasperated and determined upon revenge. So completely did they carry out their design, that in a little time it is said they killed, sacrificed, and devoured five hundred of the soldiers of Garay. Not satisfied with this, they went so far as to destroy every Spaniard whom they could find straggling, and at length took up arms for the destruction of the colony of San Estevan. Vallejo and many of his companions were killed in defending themselves, and forty Spaniards belonging to that settlement were seized and burnt in one night. Cortes immediately despatched Sandoval, with a strong force, against the Panuchese. That officer soon subdued them, making the Caciques and most of the guilty men his prisoners. Upon sending to Cortes to know what should be done with them, a message was returned that Diego de Ocampo, the magistrate, should look into the matter, and punish the guilty, while at the same time he should use all proper means to conciliate the natives. Many of the Caciques confessed their guilt, while others were proved to be guilty; and these were all either burnt or hanged. A number received a free pardon; and, that no such difficulty might occur again, the soldiers of Garay were collected and sent back to Cuba.

Cortes now turned again to the work of improvement and discovery. News having reached him that in the districts of Higueras and Honduras there were extensive and valuable mines: in fact, that gold was so plenty there, that the weights on the fishermen's nets were made of it—and, moreover, that a passage might there be discovered into the Pacific ocean—he determined to send an expedition into that region. Accordingly, he fitted out six ships, and gathering three hundred and seventy soldiers, gave the command to Christoval de Olid, with orders to proceed to Cuba, procure all necessary supplies, and thence to pursue his voyage to Higueras and make a settlement.

Troubles were still gathering for Cortes in Spain. His enemies were still active against him; the tax-gatherers who had been sent out by the King envied him his palace and his authority over the new kingdom. Private hatred, too, was in the hearts of some. One of his men (Rodrigo de Albornoz) had ambitiously desired to marry the daughter of the Prince of Tezcuco, and Cortes had opposed it.

The man remembered this with a bitter feeling. Heavy accusations against Cortes had been sent to Spain. He was charged with laying heavy taxes upon the people, fortifying castles for his own use, and in every way preparing to make himself a king. The Bishop of Burgos and Narvaez urged these accusations warmly before the King, while, as formerly, the Duke of Bejar used his influence against them; the King was wavering and undecided. At length, in an effort to please both parties, he determined that the conduct of Cortes should be investigated. Ponce de Leon was therefore despatched to Mexico, with powers to seize the Governor if he should think it necessary, and send him under a strong guard to Spain.

Difficulties at home, too, again annoyed him. Olid, upon his arrival at Cuba, tempted by Velasquez, had proved a traitor to his general. Proceeding to Higueras, he had planted the colony of the *Triumph of the Cross*, and declared himself independent of Cortes. The Spanish leader was greatly grieved over this treason. Olid had shared with him his trials and his triumphs; and yet it was necessary to punish him, as an example to the rest of his countrymen. An expedition, under the command of Francisco Las Casas, was immediately sent against him. The vessel was unfortunately driven ashore by a storm; some of the men perished, others were made prisoners by Olid—

among the rest, Las Casas. Upon being set free, however, he persuaded the soldiers of Olid to return to their duty, and seize their traitorous leader. Olid was arrested, shortly afterward sentenced to die, and beheaded.

Anxious to stop this treason, and not hearing promptly from Las Casas, Cortes had gathered his forces for a start. With a large body of Spaniards, and three thousand Mexicans, headed by their chiefs, all under the command of himself and Sandoval, he set out by land for that region. After passing Coatzacuales,* where he was received with fire-works and every demonstration of joy, his march was perhaps as perilous and trying as any adventure of his life. It lay through a wild and uninhabited country, intersected by rivers, and covered with tangled forests, which completely shut out the light of day. They were forced to construct bridges for passing the streams, and to cut their way through the thick woods that surrounded them. Starvation and disease followed in their track; they ate such roots and berries as they could find: multitudes perished. At one time Cortes was compelled to punish his soldiers for seizing and devouring some of the natives. With an undying perseverance he pushed his way on, and

* At this place they met with the brother and mother of Dona Marina. The mother, knowing her guilt, was almost afraid to meet her daughter; but Dona Marina treated her very kindly, and interceded in her behalf with Cortes.

*Audience of New Spain.** Wearied and disgusted, at length, in 1530, he left the kingdom and returned to Mexico.

Here, again, he was in the midst of disappointments. The *Audiencia*, jealous of his power, watched his every movement, while every plan proposed by him met with their decided opposition. Backed as they were by the King and his ministers in Spain, it was idle for him to oppose them. Wearied with the little meanness of these men, his thoughts turned again to the pursuits of his early life; he determined to embark in new discoveries and exploits. He had in his mind the thought that a passage might be found between the Atlantic and Pacific oceans (or the North and South seas, as they were then called) somewhere on the eastern coast of North America, or through the isthmus of Panama. Accordingly, he fitted out expeditions to attempt these discoveries, and intrusted the command to able pilots. They were, of course, unsuccessful in finding what they searched for. Disappointed in this, he now sent out various armaments from the western shores of the Mexican empire, to make discoveries in the South sea. The first, under the command of Mendoza and Mazuela, was unsuccessful. A second, in charge of Becerra, was fortunate enough to

* This government was afterward superseded by that of Viceroys.

reach the southern extremity of the rich peninsula of California; but a mutiny arising among the men, destroyed the hope of further discovery. With an untiring energy, Cortes now made ready another expedition, and took the command himself. Storms and hardships beset him in his voyage; yet, with a desperate resolution, he pressed on, reached the region discovered by Becerra,* and planted the colony of La Santa Cruz. He now returned to Mexico to procure supplies. Here difficulties again beset him, and he thought it prudent to send for his followers in the new colony and bring them home, to save them from starvation. Still resolute, however, as soon as he was able to do so he sent out another expedition, under Francisco de Ulloa. This likewise proved unfortunate. In these unprofitable enterprises it is said he spent no less than three hundred thousand crowns.

His losses, together with the continued jealousies of the Audiencia, now prompted him again to return to his native country, in the hope of finding redress. Accordingly, in 1540, he sailed homeward. Upon his arrival, he found his reception very different from what it had been before. He was now known as a disappointed adventurer. Pizarro and Almagro had been making brilliant

* It is commonly supposed that Cortes was the discoverer of California, but the author regards Diego de Becerra as the discoverer of that peninsula.

discoveries in Peru, and all thoughts were turned toward them. He was now not so much to be dreaded by the King. He treated him neither as a friend nor an enemy—worse than either, with a cold indifference. The ministers carried themselves toward him with actual scorn. Strange as it may seem, this was the treatment which the conqueror of Mexico received in his native land!

For seven tedious years did he seek redress at the court of Spain.* Day after day did he entreat for justice at the hands of those who managed the affairs of America; day after day did he demand of the King that his services should be remembered. No gratitude for those perilous services, however, could move that monarch. The man who had given to his country an empire in the New World was doomed never again to have authority in it. Nay, the King added insult to injury. It is said that on one occasion, when Cortes appeared at court, and was pressing through the crowd to approach the monarch, the King, anxious to wound him by pretending not to know him, cried out to his attendants, " Who is that person?" The answer of Cortes was direct. " Tell his Majesty," cried the conqueror, "that it is one who has conquered for him more kingdoms than his ancestors left him provinces!"

His life was well nigh ended. His continued disappointments mortified him; grief over his broken hopes preyed upon him; domestic affliction rolled in to fill the cup of his misery, and he sank under the burden. He died on the second day of December, 1547, in the sixty-second year of his age. His remains were buried with great ceremony in the chapel of the Dukes of Medina Sidonia; but, in obedience to a direction in his will, were afterward taken to the New World, and now rest in that city which he discovered and conquered, but was not allowed to rule.

THE END.